Experiments on Embryos

Should we experiment on human embryos? Should we use them, or tissue from them, for therapeutic or research programmes? These are perennially interesting and controversial questions, and the debate around them ranges from visions of new Frankenstein's monsters and grotesque hybrids on the one hand, to the possibility of cures for terrible diseases like AIDS and cancer on the other.

The contributors to this book, distinguished international figures in the field, cover the scientific, legal, ethical, theological, historical, and public policy dimensions of human embryo research and experimentation. The cases for and against embryo experiments are put strongly and clearly, and the scientific evidence is cogently presented by leading figures in embryology, including Professor Robert Edwards, one of the pioneers of the *in vitro* fertilization technique.

Anthony Dyson is Samuel Ferguson Professor of Social and Pastoral Theology and Academic Director of the Centre for Social Ethics and Policy, University of Manchester. He was a member of the Warnock Committee. John Harris is Professor of Applied Philosophy, School of Education, and Research Director of the Centre for Social Ethics and Policy, University of Manchester. He is the author of *The Value of Life* (Routledge, 1989).

Social Ethics and Policy Series

Edited by Anthony Dyson and John Harris
Centre for Social Ethics and Policy, University of Manchester

Experiments on Embryos

Edited by
Anthony Dyson
and
John Harris

ROUTLEDGE

London and New York

First published 1990 by Routledge
First published in paperback 1991 by Routledge
11 New Fetter Lane, London EC4P 4EE
29 West 35th Street, New York, NY 10001

Printed in England by Clays Ltd, St Ives plc

British Library Cataloguing in Publication Data
Experiments on Embryos
  1. Medicine. Research. Use of human embryos.
  Ethical aspects
  I. Dyson, Anthony
  II. Harris, John
  174′.28

Library of Congress Cataloging in Publication Data
Experiments on embryos/edited by Anthony Dyson & John Harris.
  p.   cm. — (Social ethics and policy series)
  Bibliography: p.
  Includes index.
  1. Human reproductive technology—Social aspects.
  2. Human reproductive technology—Moral and ethical aspects.
  3. Human embryo—Research—Social aspects.   4. Human embryo—
  Research—Moral and ethical aspects.   I. Dyson, Anthony Oakley,
  1935–
  II. Harris, John.   III. Series.
  RG133.5.E96   1989
  174′.28—dc19   89–3597

ISBN 0–415–00748–8
      0–415–00749–6 (cased)

Contents

Preface

The Centre for Social Ethics and Policy, University of Manchester, sponsors an annual public lecture series on issues of pressing public concern, Four of the contributors to this volume, Professor R. G. Edwards, Professor John Marshall, Mr D. J. Cusine, and Professor Keith Ward, were the lecturers for 1987 on the theme: 'The ethical issues of embryo research'. Such was the interest in the lecture series, and indeed in the topic, that we decided to commission essays not only from the four lecturers, but from others who have an interest in this field. The result, we hope, is a balanced set of contributions covering the scientific, legal, ethical, theological, historical, and policy dimensions of human embryo research and experimentation.

A.O.D. and J.M.H.
Centre for Social Ethics and Policy
University of Manchester, 1989.

Acknowledgements

The editors are grateful to the many people who have helped to make possible this volume. In particular, Ms Gillian Shepherd's assistance with the production of the volume has been invaluable. Our colleagues Dr Mary Lobjoit, Professor Mark Ferguson, and Dr Dian Donnai have been invaluable and generous sources of medical and scientific advice which as 'lay-persons' we have probably frequently misunderstood. We are grateful to Professor John Turner, Professor Iain Gillespie, and Professor Jean MacFarlane, for their stimulating chairmanship of the original lecture series and finally we owe a special debt to our fellow directors of the Centre for Social Ethics and Policy, Mary Lobjoit and Margaret Brazier, for their constant support and encouragement.

Notes on contributors

Margaret Brazier is Professor of Law, and Legal Studies Director of the Centre for Social Ethics and Policy, University of Manchester. She is the author of *Medicine, Patients and the Law* (1987).

Douglas J. Cusine is Senior Lecturer and Head of Department, Department of Conveyancing and Professional Practice of Law, University of Aberdeen. He has written extensively on law and medicine.

Anthony Dyson is Samuel Ferguson Professor of Social and Pastoral Theology, Faculty of Theology, University of Manchester. He chairs the University of Manchester Committee on the Ethics of Research on Human Beings and was a member of The Warnock Committee.

Robert Edwards is Professor of Human Reproduction, University of Cambridge. He was the pioneer, with Patrick Steptoe, of the *in vitro* fertilization techniques which led to the birth of the first 'test-tube baby'.

Mark W. J. Ferguson is Professor of Basic Dental Sciences and Head of the Department of Cell and Structural Biology, University of Manchester. He is internationally known for his research into normal and cleft palate development.

John Harris is Professor of Applied Philosophy in the Department of Education, University of Manchester. He is the author of *Violence and Responsibility* (1980), *The Value of Life* (1985), and co-editor of *Consent and the Incompetent Patient* (1988).

John Marshall is Professor of Clinical Neurology, University of London. He was a member of The Warnock Committee and of the Papal Commission prior to *Humanae Vitae*.

Keith Ward is Professor of History and Philosophy of Religion, King's College, London University. His books include *Rational Theology and the Creativity of God* (1982).

Edward Yoxen is Lecturer in the Department of Science and Technology Policy, University of Manchester. He is author of *The Gene Business* (1983) and *Unnatural Selection* (1986).

Introduction

The question of whether or not we should experiment on embryos or use them, or tissue or cells from them, for therapeutic or research purposes is one that will not go away. Indeed, the United Kingdom Government has recently asked this question for the second time. On the first occasion they commissioned The Warnock Committee to provide an answer. This was duly delivered in July 1984 and it has been hotly debated ever since. Perhaps in consequence of the continued debate the question was re-asked by the Department of Health and Social Security in the form of a consultation paper published in December 1986. The debate is still going on and indeed it is quite clear that it will not be quelled by legislation. For this is not the sort of debate that is susceptible of a final answer. Partly of course because we will never have a complete view of the uses to which human embryos may be put, and hence we will never have a final account of the arguments which might be used to justify, and perhaps make apparently imperative, their use for the sake of humankind. Nor, of course, and for the same reasons, will we ever have a final account of the purported refutations of those arguments and claims.

In the meanwhile, we can hope to see a little less darkly into the problems and the issues that underlie the question of whether or not we should permit experiments on embryos. It is with this hope that the present collection of essays has been assembled.

It is easy to take a firm stand. Indeed many discussions of the vexed question which is the theme of this volume start with their conclusions and then work their way logically back to the arguments that will sustain those conclusions. However, before taking a stand for or against experiments on embryos, it is as well to have a clear view of just what one might be deciding to permit or indeed to deny oneself and, for that matter, to deny one's fellows.

Mark Ferguson, writing as a cell biologist well acquainted with contemporary scientific research and aware of what is and may be possible in the field, examines just what is happening in science at the moment, and, more importantly perhaps, looks ahead to what may be done and achieved if embryo research is not outlawed. Ferguson explores the full range of research in embryology, from the immense task of mapping the 3,500 million base pairs that comprise the complete set of genes we humans possess – the human genome, to the advantages of operating on individual cells to cure or prevent particular diseases. He considers the possibilities and the limitations of such things as genetic engineering and the creation of new life forms and comments on which may really be possibilities and which are sheer science fantasy. Ferguson's chapter sets the stage for the ethical debate that is to follow.

Robert Edwards, as joint 'father', with Patrick Steptoe, of the first test-tube baby, Louise Brown, born over a decade ago now, has also a claim to be regarded as one of the fathers of modern embryology. In his contribution to this volume, Edwards takes us through a short history of the developments in embryology which he has pioneered and sets the stage for the work of the next decade. Edwards' paper is especially interesting in that it not only provides an account of the latest developments from one of the leading figures in the field, but is the personal testament of a working scientist setting out the ethical principles which govern his approach to his own research in this controversial area. Edwards both explains the personal limits he sets himself in working on human embryos and argues for a flexible but strictly controlled limit to permissible research. He patiently explains just why The Warnock Committee's recommendations are inappropriate and suggests that, far from being concerned about fertilized eggs or embryos, it might well be the gametes that prove more important in the long term.

Whereas Ferguson and Edwards are concerned with the present and the future, Edward Yoxen argues that there is value in looking at present-day concerns about research activity on embryos in historical perspective. It is usual to think of interest in the ethics of embryo research as arising from the dramatic developments of *in vitro* fertilization which focused on the birth of Louise Brown. It is salutary to be reminded that research activity on embryos raising ethical questions antedates *in vitro* fertilization by centuries. The increase in, and publicity about, experiments on embryos does not fully explain the degree of public disquiet and opposition that these experiments occasion. Explanations of this should probably be sought in the political climate and through resultant changes in moral sensibility. Yoxen examines two pioneering studies of an earlier generation – Needham's *A History of Embryology* and Corner's *Ourselves Unborn; An Embryologist's Essay on Man* – and then goes on to review the historical tradition from the early Middle Ages down to modern developments. Yoxen contends that, in evaluating human embryo research, we should attend primarily to the rights and feelings of the women who make it possible.

John Marshall's chapter presents a reasoned case against embryo research. Writing as both a medical practitioner and a scientist Professor Marshall first makes clear what is meant by research and then goes on to examine the way in which a researcher's disposition to describe what she or he is doing in a particular way will undoubtedly influence her or his assessment of the moral character of what she or he is doing. Marshall's central thesis is that the question of when human life begins is not (as it appears) a scientific question, nor a biological question, but rather a philosophical question with theological overtones.

Marshall identifies the potential of the embryo to become a full human being as crucial to the solution of this philosophical question. His argument stems from a reverence for all life and a consciousness of its unique importance. He links our attitudes to embryo research with the general respect for life and for the environment and argues that, in view of this respect, the use of embryos for therapeutic purposes and for research is not the way forward for humankind.

Any discussion of the ethics of embryo experimentation would have to address the crucial problem of the moral status of the fetus. John Harris argues that this problem must be settled before any conclusions can be reached about the justification of such practices as experiments on embryos or the use of embryonic organs or tissue. Harris reviews some of the principal positions that may be taken on the question of what precisely this status is or on whether or not embryos have rights, and concluded that at no stage in the three trimesters of normal embryonic development does the embryo attain a moral significance which would demand that it be protected and accorded rights comparable to those possessed, for example, by adult human beings.

The chapter then explores the relationship between deeply held feelings and moral principles and argues that feelings cannot be accorded moral priority. The benefits to be expected from embryo research are briefly rehearsed and the question is posed as to whether the benefits that accrue to individuals or to society from permitting abortions, for example, are greater than those expected from embryo research. Harris concludes that the benefits from embryo research substantially outweigh the dangers, and that, in the absence of compelling argument for the protection of the embryo, this work should be permitted.

Some of the main Christian Churches in Great Britain have been conspicuously active in the debate which has followed The Warnock Report. By and large, their pronouncements have been unsympathetic to the prospect of embryo research. Anthony Dyson presents a critical analysis of these theological contributions, against a shifting cultural background in which science and technology are losing their former pre-eminent status. Dyson looks at the different ways in which the denominational traditions use their resources of the Bible, tradition, natural law, experience, knowledge, and reason. He identifies three major problems: uncritical interpretation of the Biblical writings and of writings in the subsequent tradition; the doubtful validity of natural law in the way it is commonly used; and the lack of proper attention to the claims of experience and knowledge. Given the many variables, theological ethics may not claim to settle the ethical issues of embryo research. But, by overcoming endemic individualism with a doctrine of interdependence and by developing a notion of 'posterity', it is possible to make out a stronger case for embryo research than many Church pronouncements will allow.

Keith Ward discusses mainly philosophical and ethical issues raised by experimentation on embryos. He considers four areas where there are basic disputes of an irresolvable nature. The first relates to verificationism, which says that there must be ways of getting agreement at least on all factual matters by observation; this position is opposed by a natural kinds theorist. The second area concerns personal identity; here we can contrast a dualist view with a non-dualist view. The third area relates to how morality is ultimately founded; here the utilitarian takes human preferences as the basis of all ethical decisions, whereas the absolutist judges that there are final limits on human action which must never be overridden. The fourth area concerns the role of nature and human responsibility. On the one hand, we are responsible for what we do in the world; we must aim to bring about what is good, regardless of what the processes of nature do. Against this, it is objected that it is always wrong to frustrate a purpose of nature. All these four areas being contestable, we are faced with a 'vital living and forced option' to make a decision, to commit ourselves absolutely in objective uncertainty. Ward concludes that philosophical ethics may bring increased understanding, increased concern for rationality, and increased clarity and self-knowledge; it will never bring agreement.

There are two chapters by lawyers. The first is by Douglas Cusine who regards embryo research as the crucial issue faced by The Warnock Committee. After outlining the principal arguments for and against, Cusine turns to specifically legal matters. At present there is not much law in this area and it is difficult to extrapolate from other areas to fill this gap. If legal protection for the embryo is required, the embryo may at the moment be regarded as an item of property. We have to reckon with abuse of *in vitro* fertilization and research, so some legislative clarification is needed as a matter of urgency. The Warnock agenda could have been foreseen a decade and a half ago. Legislation would have to reconcile two viewpoints, namely the desire to advance scientific knowledge and the necessity to work within society's existing moral framework. Cusine is strongly in favour of the Licensing Authority proposed by Warnock, but believes it should include a lawyer and some members of the general public among its number. Research on the embryo could be carried out for up to fourteen days; the Licensing Authority would have power to vary that limit. Overall, he concludes, the need for legislation is urgent. 'The last thing we want is darkness, legislatively speaking, for another five years.'

Finally, Margaret Brazier analyses the British Government's current proposals for regulating embryo experimentation in the White Paper of 1987. The options placed before Parliament are critically examined and certain inconsistencies are exposed. Thus it is argued that Option A prohibiting research does not in reality assert the full humanity of the embryo. Option B is seen to be a compromise with only a dubious rational basis. The nature of the embryo is at the heart of the debate on both abortion and embryo research. This chapter explores what legal consequences should properly result from that unresolved and irresolvable debate, and suggests that it does not necessarily follow that if embryo research is banned the present abortion laws must also be repealed. The disputed status of the embryo demands that the law afford it protection but not at the expense of the mother, whose full humanity is unchallengeable. Feminist objections to research are growing and the basis of some feminist concern about research is discussed. Finally, the practicality of the Government's proposals is examined and the initial reactions of Members of Parliament are looked at.

Chapter one

Contemporary and future possibilities for human embryonic manipulation

Mark W. J. Ferguson

Introduction

This chapter describes current possibilities for the manipulation of human embryos and speculates on likely future developments in this area. It focuses on what is, or could be, feasible in scientific terms and attempts to analyse, from an objective standpoint, what could or could not be done. It makes no attempt to consider the ethics of such manipulations, nor to address whether such manipulations should be performed. It also addresses some earlier speculations about future possibilities in the field of human embryonic manipulation from the standpoint of analysing whether they are scientifically possible or impossible.

This chapter does not consider possible advances in techniques, for example improvements in methods of recovering eggs, of fertilizing them *in vitro* and replacing them in the mother, or improvements in the screening of sperm or in the *in vitro* culture conditions. I have no doubt that major advances will be made in these areas and that they will have a significant clinical impact, particularly for the treatment of infertile couples. However, from the perspective of this book, they pose few new ethical problems. Instead they are merely better ways of doing the same thing, with a greater chance of success. For this reason, detailed consideration of such advances is outside the scope of a chapter whose aim is to lay the scientific framework for future ethical debate.

It must also be emphasized that many of the manipulations of human embryonic development which I will describe do not necessarily require *in vitro* fertilization. It would, for example, be theoretically possible to recover early fertilized human eggs, to conduct such manipulations, and then to reimplant them into the mother. However, the logistics of such operations are quite mind-blowing and it therefore seems likely that such manipulations will be conducted on embryos derived from *in vitro* fertilization protocols.

The point is worth making however, because there is a distinction between discussing the ethics of *in vitro* fertilization *per se*, and the ethics of human embryonic manipulation which does not of necessity depend upon *in vitro* fertilization, but which is technically facilitated by it, and is likely to be the only logistical way of conducting such manipulations on a wide scale.

I am also acutely aware of the problems surrounding future speculations. On the one hand there is the argument that if you can predict it, the advance will probably not be very important, as most major advances break new ground in areas which people had not previously considered. On the other hand, some of the possibilities which I predict may turn out to be unachievable and I feel certain that I have failed to predict at least some major future therapies. Nonetheless, I believe that there is value in trying rationally to assess what may be scientifically achievable so that at least the ethics of such procedures might be considered.

Prenatal diagnosis

Advances in the prenatal diagnosis of many genetic disorders have accelerated markedly in the past few years. In early days chromosomal analysis and certain biochemical tests were the mainstay of the prenatal diagnosis. All that has now changed with the advent of numerous genetic probes to detect the presence or absence of a large number of normal or mutated genes within the genome. These genetic probes have opened up a whole new horizon for the early detection of human disease and disease susceptibilities. First, the probes are very specific and can be used to detect precisely small defined aberrations in genotype. It seems highly likely that large panels of these gene probes will be available within the next few years; already many are available. Second, accompanying the explosion in human genetic probes has been a corresponding development of the technology for obtaining large enough quantities of host DNA to conduct such analyses. It is now possible to take a single cell, extract the DNA from it and then, if one knows the region of the genome one wishes to examine, to amplify up that region to obtain enough DNA for analysis by gene probing. Currently there are some diseases which are diagnosable using the quantity of DNA present in a single cell. This technology is rapidly expanding and it seems likely that nearly all future diagnoses could be made on the basis of a single cell biopsy.

Such technology now means that single cell biopsy of early human embryos growing by *in vitro* fertilization techniques is a possibility. This DNA could be amplified and screened using a panel of DNA probes in order to detect the presence or absence of a variety of normal or mutated genes. This opens up two further possibilities. First, a panel of embryos generated by *in vitro* fertilization could be screened and the 'best' one returned to the mother for reimplantation and further development. Second, specific gene therapy to correct various genetic defects is achievable (see later) as embryos carrying such genetic defects can now be detected.

At first sight this seems a relatively straightforward issue largely because gene probes are currently available for some of the major genetic diseases. In the future, therefore, it may be possible to detect at an early stage such disorders as Huntington's chorea, cystic fibrosis, cleft lip and palate, spina bifida, etc. However, much progress is now being made on elucidating the genetic basis of a large number of other diseases, including susceptibilities to disorders which involve a genetic and environmental component, e.g. cancer. Moreover, the development of a genetic and physical map followed by complete sequencing of the estimated 3,500 million base pairs making up the human genome are now technically feasible: all that is required is the will and the money (about 50 pence per base pair). The time estimated to complete this massive task varies from 3 to 30 years, depending upon the international resources devoted to the project; the ever-increasing sophistication of DNA sequencing machines is likely to reduce the time and the cost in financial and man-hour terms.

In parallel with this task will be an explosion in the mapping of particular genes to various regions of the genome, a greater understanding of chromosomal organization and gene control, and a solid database of genetic susceptibilities to various disease states and how these may interact with the environment. Having mapped the genome once, it is likely that techniques will evolve for the rapid sequencing of important areas of individual human genomes. This being so, there is every reason to believe that inside 50 to 100 years every human being could have his genome (or at least important regions of it) mapped either at birth or as a very early embryo. Individual genetic defects and susceptibilities to various diseases would then be known. Preventative health care strategies could be evolved for individuals on the basis of their known genetic susceptibilities.

This opens up very wide-ranging possibilities for the screening of embryos to be reimplanted as part of an *in vitro* fertilization programme. Embryos could not only be screened for the major genetic diseases but also for a variety of other parameters including such things as susceptibility to adult cancers, infections, etc. Different embryos will show widely differing profiles of susceptibility or resistance to various disorders when such widespread screening is applied. Therefore decisions about which embryos to reimplant will be all the more complex. Indeed, it seems likely that the number of embryos fertilized *in vitro* would be the rate-limiting step in any kind of purposeful selection experiment. The variation between embryos is likely to be so great that one would have to screen thousands, if not millions, of embryos from individual couples if one were to attempt deliberately to select certain consistent genotypes on a population basis. I therefore have no fears about the potential to manipulate the human gene pool (for good or bad); the sheer numbers required to achieve this precludes it as a rational possibility. I also believe that natural selection has left much to be desired, in terms of the human gene pool, and individual selections at this level are unlikely to have any detrimental effects, only advantageous ones. Therefore, scaremongering based on manipulation of the human gene pool by sophisticated screening is unjustified.

What is, however, justified is a consideration of how decisions will be made concerning which embryos to reimplant, given the likely range and sophistication of available prenatal tests. With the limited numbers of embryos generated by *in vitro* fertilization it seems probable that each of these embryos (like those generated by conventional reproductive strategies) will have problems in some area or another. The decision will therefore be one of trade-offs. Who will help the couple to decide which embryos to reimplant, given a perplexing number of trade-offs in relation to likely susceptibilities to adult diseases? What criteria should we use to make these decisions?

These genetic probes could be used not only to screen for disease susceptibilities, but also for likely adult phenotypes such as sex, height, etc. Much scaremongering has abounded about the possibility of manipulating the sex ratio of the human species. However, it should be remembered that this possibility already exists: a mother may have an amniocentesis during her pregnancy, determine the sex of the fetus, and elect to have an abortion if it is not of the desired sex; societies may practise sexually selective infanticide. In fact, selection of the sex of the embryo is much more likely to be achieved by selection of sperm. Techniques are already being developed which allow the separation of future male- and female-determining sperm from a variety of domestic animals. It seems likely that such techniques will improve in the next few years and may be applied to the human situation. Logically the easiest way to manipulate the sex of the embryo is not by genetic screening of embryos developing by *in vitro* fertilization, but rather by selection of the sperm, and artificial insemination *in vivo* or selective

9

fertilization *in vitro*. In the latter, all the embryos fertilized *in vitro* (or at least a high percentage of them) would be of the desired sex and these could then be screened using gene probes for major disorders, etc; this is the most logical approach given that the number of embryos generated will be the rate-limiting step in screening for the best one to reimplant (see earlier).

Such developments highlight another likely possibility, namely better criteria for the selection of ova and sperm for the *in vitro* fertilization procedure. It may be possible to extend such selection beyond such parameters as likely fertilizing capacity, potential to grow *in vitro*, potential to reimplant, etc., to cover characteristics which may be displayed in the embryo. This is an area which has currently not been explored using genetic probes but if techniques were available for the removal of small pieces of DNA from ova or sperm and their replacement after screening, then it might be possible genetically to screen the gametes and make rational predictions about the likely outcome after fertilization. I believe this is a theoretical scientific possibility, but is probably a long way off. At the present time it seems likely that the sheer logistics and technical effort required would indicate that ova and sperm would be screened only using crude parameters leaving the more sophisticated investigations of genetic constitution to a later stage when they would be dealt with by single cell biopsy of the embryo followed by screening using a number of gene probes.

It has also been suggested that *in vitro* fertilization programmes may be used to create banks of good embryos generated when the mother is in peak reproductive performance which could then be reimplanted, should the mother so desire, later in life when the natural risk of such disorders as Down's syndrome are much higher. Certainly there is some sense in this proposal, particularly in relationship to age-related chromosomal or genetic aberrations of the embryo such as Down's syndrome. However, it is well known that the maternal environment, e.g. the amount of blood flow to the uterus, the nutrition of the embryo, the volume of amniotic fluid, etc., all play a major role in successful fetal outcome. It is unclear how well the ageing human female reproductive system would cope with such good embryos. For certain, they would not have the major malformations like Down's syndrome, but perhaps they would be less than optimal in their development. I would therefore only see such techniques being applied when there was some pressing need for the mother to be pregnant in later years. Its use is therefore likely to be limited. One would certainly not advocate such procedures for the routine delaying of pregnancy, e.g. until the mother had achieved a suitable prominence in her career. Such widespread voluntary practices would be contraindicated (a) because of the likely poor environment for the embryo in the ageing female reproductive system, and (b) because of the simple fact that the older you are when you produce children, the less time you are likely to have (in terms of life expectancy and quality of life) to bring them up to an age at which they become independent.

Somatic line manipulations

A somatic line manipulation would involve alteration (e.g. of the genes) of the cells of an individual embryo so as to, for example, correct a genetic defect. This manipulation would be limited to the cells of that individual embryo and would not be passed on to its offspring. This is in contradistinction to a germ line manipulation (see later) which would alter the genome not only of that individual embryo but also of its offspring.

It follows that if one can detect genetic disorders in early embryos then some of these could be corrected. Thus, for example, if a particular gene was deleted in an individual embryo this gene could be reinserted into the correct stem cell line thus correcting the genetic defect and preventing a major adult handicap. Techniques exist for the introduction of specific pieces of DNA into cells (see later): such manipulations are therefore currently possible and most likely to be utilized for straightforward single gene defects.

Moreover, somatic line manipulations may not necessarily involve interference with the early embryonic genome. Instead the manipulation may be at the cellular level. Thus, for example, early embryos which had abnormal cells could have these removed, either surgically or by killing them using toxins coupled to specific monoclonal antibodies which specifically recognized those abnormal cells. More likely would be the introduction of additional cellular material to make an embryonic chimera. For example, if the embryo were deficient in cells making a particular type of hormone or particular blood cells, then stem cells for such components could be introduced into the embryo to correct the defect.

This raises two questions. First, the source of the donated cells: this matter is dealt with in a later section on embryonic/fetal transplantations. Second, the likely stage of development at which such manipulations would take place. It seems likely that most somatic line cellular manipulations would occur in later embryos or fetuses and as such the manipulations are likely to be carried out on embryos regardless of whether or not they have been fertilized *in vitro* or by conventional *in vivo* mechanisms. Such procedures have already been performed on human embryos (see later section on embryonic/fetal transplantations).

Germ line manipulations

Unlike somatic line manipulations germ line manipulations are likely to be almost exclusively at the DNA level. In recent years the technology for such genetic manipulations has advanced dramatically in experimental animals and I first provide a summary of such technology and how it is being used in animals, before describing how it could be used in the human situation.

It must be made clear that construction of transgenic animals is currently a fairly difficult laboratory procedure and that the difficulties increase as one ascends the vertebrate kingdom. It seems likely, therefore, that there will be some problems to be solved before the first human transgenic can be made. However, scientifically I believe that this ought to be possible within the next five years if not before.

A transgenic animal (or plant) is one whose genetic composition has been altered to include selected DNA sequences from another organism by methods other than those used in conventional animal breeding, i.e. transgenic animals contain non-parental DNA. In the animal kingdom, production of such transgenic animals has opened up whole new lines of experimental investigation including the analysis of gene expression in the tissues of the intact animal rather than in tissue culture systems. It has also opened up many potential beneficial applications of these organisms in the production of compounds or tissue for human use. Recently in the United States it has been ruled that transgenic animals can be patented as a new life form and the whole technology now has a heavy commercial investment.

The most usual method for introducing the non-parental DNA is by injection into one of the pronuclei of the early embryo. Such techniques are relatively straightforward in mice but more difficult in domestic species such as sheep, cows, pigs, and probably in man.

Two new methods of introducing the non-parental DNA are undergoing rapid development. The first involves modified retro viruses to deliver the non-parental DNA into the chromosomes of the embryo. The second uses genetically manipulated totipotential[1] cells (e.g. embryonic stem cells derived from early embryos or from embryonal teratocarcinomas)[2] which are introduced into the early embryo to form a chimera: the offspring of such cells contributing to the various tissues of the developing embryo.

These transgenic organisms provide a powerful new tool for investigating basic scientific questions such as how oncogenes (genes which may be involved in cancer development) co-operate and complement each other; the tracing of embryonic cell lineages (i.e.

what cells in the adult are derived from what pieces of the embryo); the tissue specific expression of certain genes (i.e. why certain types of cells only develop in certain regions of the body); the development of the body pattern (i.e. how tissues such as the hand and foot, both of which are composed of identical tissues – bone, cartilage, muscle, skin, etc. – come to have different patterns); and the co-ordination and regulation of growth.

Transgenic techniques have also enabled investigators to develop new strains of organism of benefit to the agricultural and medical industries. These include:

- the ability to produce pharmacologically important compounds in novel, easily accessible body compartments, e.g. the production of clotting factor nine[3] in the sheep mammary gland, where it can be extracted from the milk;
- the production of organisms genetically resistant to disease (to overcome problems of vaccination or, more importantly, diseases where no vaccine exists);
- the development of more efficient domesticated livestock, e.g. to get animals to grow bigger, faster and at a higher food conversion ratio without upsetting the physiological balance (such procedures have been achieved by engineering growth hormone releasing factor genes to be overexpressed in various animals);
- the production of animals capable of existing in an adverse environment (e.g. by engineering in genes which confer resistance to certain environmental pullutants such as heavy metals);
- the development of better animal models for human disease (e.g. a better mouse model for mammary gland cancer) or the development of animal models for human diseases where no comparable disease exists in animal populations (e.g. muscular dystrophy or Lesch-Nyhan syndrome).

The major advantage in producing a transgenic animal is that the manipulation is undertaken on the germ line. Thus once a suitable gene has been engineered into the animal and found to be expressed in an advantageous way, that animal stock can be maintained by conventional breeding. At the present time there is variation in terms of the stability of the genetic insert, i.e. some inserted genes remain permanently integrated within the host genome and seem to be capable of indefinite transmission via conventional breeding, whereas others are lost after a certain number of breedings (unstable inserts). Much current research is focusing on the factors which make these genetic inserts stable or unstable.

Effectively, by this mechanism one can create a whole new type of animal very quickly. Interestingly, the major investment in terms of time and effort is in screening the transgenic animals created and in the breeding programme. The DNA and *in vitro* fertilization technology, whilst complex, is not nearly so time-consuming. For experimental investigators the big investment is in the animal house!

The technology for germ line manipulation therefore exists. The question is, how could it be applied to the human embryo? I see two broad areas of application – corrective modification and positive modification.

Corrective modification

Individuals diagnosed as having single gene defects could have them corrected by insertion of the appropriate gene. Unlike somatic line manipulations these insertions would be heritable, i.e. the defect would be corrected not only in the individual but also in his or her offspring. With increasing development of the technique not only would replacement gene therapy be possible, but also therapy for quantitative gene expression. Thus it may be possible to correct disorders where genes are not expressed in the right place at the right time or in the right amount. Currently single gene replacement therapy is feasible; multiple gene replacement and other developments could be predicted for the future.

Positive modification

Under this strategy one would manipulate the embryo so as to engineer into it additional genes which, for example, may not naturally occur in the human species. Thus the manipulation would not be to correct a natural genetic defect but rather to insert wholly new genes. This remains a future possibility. There are numerous difficulties in constructing genes which can be inserted into an animal to obtain the correct expression of the gene in the right tissues at the right time. The issue is not simple even for straightforward proteins such as factor nine being produced in the milk of sheep.

Nonetheless, as our knowledge of targeting DNA insertions into the genome and of tissue, and stage-specific gene expression increases, and tissue-specific promotors become available, I believe that it will soon be possible to insert different genes into the human genome. Such therapy could be wholly advantageous. For example, it may be possible to insert individual genes coding for antibodies against all the major infections, including hepatitis B, malaria, AIDS, etc., or to insert genes which code for enzymes which would destroy carcinogens or environmental pollutants, or for genes which would repair DNA and so retard ageing, or even to engineer in biosensor genes. In the latter technique one could insert a gene which would cause a colourful protein to be excreted in the urine once the level of a particular molecule within the body (e.g. an oncogene protein which is precancerous) reached a certain threshold level. In other words, when your urine turned green, you would know that you were about to develop a malignant tumour in your lung and could go straight away to hospital for early corrective treatment of that cancer.

Such ideas are rather futuristic but do signal a major new way in which the human species could adapt to a rapidly changing environment. Such positive gene therapy would be a powerful directed alternative to random gene mutation and natural selection which, as I indicated earlier, leave much to be desired. It may be extremely useful for protection of certain individuals against various environmental pollutants and major new infections such as AIDS.

However, it must be emphasized that this positive therapy can only be conducted on individual embryos. Therefore, to achieve any kind of population effect would require a very dramatic change in the social behaviour of human beings. As I stated earlier, the major investment (in terms of time) in animal transgenic programmes is in the animal house in the breeding programme. This would also be true for man. Thus to achieve major effects on a population basis would require:

(a) that most or all individuals reproduced by *in vitro* fertilization with transgenic manipulation of their embryos,
(b) that most, if not all individuals, abstained from reproduction by the conventional means,
(c) the careful monitoring of the transgenic embryos produced and in some cases selective mating of the transgenic adults in an organized breeding programme.

The above statements appear bizarre but are scientifically what would be required to affect a major population change in the gene pool, e.g. to engineer in a gene for resistance against infections or environmental pollutants. Given the sheer simplicity, effectiveness, and indeed pleasure of normal sexual reproduction, it appears highly unlikely that these measures could be imposed on a population basis. Moreover, the medical and technical logistics of instituting such a programme of widespread human *in vitro* fertilization and transgenic manipulation are enormous. Such considerations are therefore likely to limit the application of transgenic procedures to individual cases of corrective or positive gene therapy.

Much has been made, by way of scaremongering, of the capability of transgenic technology in the hands of evil dictators or the like who would wish to manipulate individuals' personality, intelligence, or work capacity, etc. To my mind such considerations are pure fiction from a scientific standpoint. First, in order to achieve such objectives it would be necessary to have the massive population manipulation and breeding programme I have just outlined. This would require legislation against reproduction by normal means, compulsory *in vitro* fertilization and transgenic manipulation, and in some areas compulsory first generation breeding. Such legislation would be impossible to enforce and therefore manipulation of the population for some evil intent likewise impossible. Moreover even cursory examination of the problem reveals that most political leaders want quick results and even if transgenic manipulation could be achieved in all of the population for just one year, it would take at least eighteen years for this manipulation to have any effect at the polls or indeed until any kind of breeding programme could be introduced. This long time-frame makes the evil manipulation of transgenic technology extremely remote. Moreoever, if we have succeeded in keeping our freedom in the age of mass communication by newspaper, satellite television, radio and telephone, and in a prolonged system of state education, I doubt very much if anything in the age of genetic engineering will encroach on such freedom. It should also be noted that the traits which one would wish to manipulate for evil intent, such as personality or intelligence, etc., are highly complex and involve the interaction of multiple genes and multiple environmental factors. Therefore, it seems almost impossible that these traits could be predictably altered in a specific direction by transgenic manipulation.

All of the above considerations also indicate why it is extraordinarily unlikely that any bizarre experimenter would wish to conduct transgenic experiments on 'available' human embryos as opposed to animal embryos. The long time to reproductive maturity and the complexity of the breeding programmes involved make the human species a very unsuitable model for experimental transgenic investigations. Experimenters will want to (and do) use species with a short age to reproductive maturity (e.g. mice), so facilitating large breeding programmes.

Embryonic/fetal transplantations

The use of embryonic or fetal cells or tissues to transplant into other embryos or fetuses or adults is a current reality: experiments have been done on animals and manipulations have occurred in man. The first point to make on this subject is that such fetal therapy can be conducted regardless of *in vitro* fertilization techniques. In many instances the cells or tissues of choice have to come from embryos or fetuses which are much older than the age to which human embryos can currently be developed *in vitro*. Theoretically it is possible that embryos derived from *in vitro* fertilization procedures could be grown up to the maximum stage and then the required cells or tissues removed and further grown in cell or organ culture until they were at the correct stage for transplantation. Pragmatically, however, it is much easier to remove such cells or tissues from embryos undergoing elective or therapeutic abortion. Two major types of transplant situation can be envisaged.

Embryo to adult

In this situation embryonic cells or tissues would be introduced into the adult human in order to correct for some failing system. In the simplest case, hormone secreting cells might be introduced to colonize a particular gland where the existing cells were either malfunctioning or had been destroyed. Such considerations would apply to diseases like diabetes and thyroid deficiency. In other circumstances grafts of tissues may be placed so as to restore some kind of function, as for example in the grafting of embryonic nervous tissue cells into the brains of adult humans to restore neurotransmitter function in particular areas. Both these types of manipulation have been conducted in experimental animals and in some cases already in man. Moreover, in experimental animals whole organ transplants have been conducted from late fetuses into adults. Thus, transplantation of the fetal liver or indeed the fetal heart or kidney may be conducted so as to augment the function of a failing adult organ. In these cases the transplant is not replacive, as in the conventional adult to adult transplant, but rather is additional to the failing adult organ, i.e. a supplementary transplant. Experiments in animals have shown that such transplants are highly successful. As the adult organ fails, so the fetal organ develops and begins to take over the function; moreover the surgery is nowhere near as traumatic as replacive transplants. It seems likely that increasing use will be made of fetal cells or tissues to replace or augment failing or diseased adult tissues. Such considerations have brought their own set of ethical problems, such as the diagnosis of death in an embryo, and the ethics of keeping alive human embryos which are incompatible with life after birth (e.g. anencephaly) so that valuable tissues might develop and be removed for adult transplantation.

There are several properties of embryonic cells which make them particularly useful for transplantation into adults. First, the cells possess remarkable capacity for colonizing, invading, and differentiating in adult organs. Thus they are capable of taking over the adult function. Second, and more importantly, it appears that if cells are removed from early embryos and grown for some time *in vitro* they lose some of their histocompatibility transplantation antigens, which means that the cells are not rejected by the host organism. In animal experiments it has been possible to take embryonic cells and transplant them across major species barriers such as between rats and mice or chickens and quail, not merely between individuals within a given species. Currently much research is focusing on the regulation of histocompatibility antigen expression in cells and their development in embryos. It seems likely that techniques will evolve which will allow the removal and culture of embryonic cells for transplantation into any human.

This raises the possibility of banks of embryonic cells, and two interesting implications for ethical considerations of *in vitro* fertilization. First, it seems likely that these modified embryonic cells would be derived from early embryos (perhaps transgenically modified) produced utilizing an *in vitro* fertilization scheme. It is not known whether these cells would remain viable in culture indefinitely but this seems unlikely. Therefore, a continuing supply of such cells would be required. Consideration could be given to the utilization of experimental or spare embryos derived from *in vitro* fertilization programmes for these purposes.

Second, much has been made of the possibility of cloning early embryos and freezing down some of the clones, so that they would exist as an individual bank of cells to be utilized when required by the one embryo allowed to develop into an adult. The argument has been that these embryonic cells would have the same genotype as the adult and so would not be rejected. Whilst this remains a plausible scientific possibility, it seems likely that the extensive procedures involved in cloning, and the attendant risks, would make it a less optimal strategy than developing a communal bank of transplantation antigen-free cells for use by everyone: after all, this is one of the major advantages of using embryonic tissue.

I deal with some of the current fictional notions concerning cloning later in this chapter. Suffice it to say that cloning of individual embryos and freezing the spare clones as a spare part bank for the embryo when it becomes an adult is a less likely logistical possibility than establishing large banks of non-antigenic embryonic cells from pooled embryos derived from *in vitro* fertilization procedures. This latter future possibility is not only logistically easier but also makes this material available to the population at large, i.e. not just those individuals who have been cloned and produced by *in vitro* fertilization, who are in any case likely to be few in number.

Embryo/fetus to embryo/fetus

Not only is transplantation of embryonic or fetal material to adults achievable but so too is transplantation to other embryos or fetuses. I have illustrated earlier how embryos may be somatically modified by the introduction of, for example, stem cells from another embryo to correct for deficiencies in, for example, blood cell production. The increasing sophistication of prenatal ultrasonic diagnosis now means that it is possible to detect embryos or fetuses with structural malformations very shortly after such malformations have occurred. This means that direct fetal therapy is possible. Such fetal therapy may involve administration of compounds such as amniotic fluid replacement or fetal blood transfusion; fetal surgery – either simple repair or insertion of a prosthesis (e.g. repair of cleft lip and cleft palate or spina bifida; the insertion of a drain into the brain in cases of hydrocephaly; the insertion of a shunt into the kidneys in the case of hydronephrosis); or transplantations of organs or cells into the embryo. All of these have been conducted in experimental animals and many have been conducted in man: there are numerous cases of human amniotic fluid replacement, human embryonic blood transfusion, and fetal surgery for hydrocephaly and hydronephrosis. Indeed at the present time in some of these areas more work has been done on human embryos than on animal embryos. This is for the very justifiable reason that in the absence of any kind of therapy such embryos would die. Therefore, any kind of intervention to save the embryo can be justified.

However, the early experience with placing embryonic shunts to correct for human hydrocephaly has been unrewarding. Poor selection of fetuses for surgery resulted in only the more severe cases of hydrocephaly being treated. When the results were analysed it transpired that what the fetal therapy had done was to save fetuses which would otherwise have died *in utero*, but the effect was to bring into existence thoroughly moribund individuals requiring extensive institutionalized care and whose quality of life was judged to be low. Experience with these early cases has now led to much more careful selection of fetuses and only those who are mildly affected by hydrocephalus would be treated to prevent mental retardation. However, when the past experiences of such fetal therapies are presented to a woman with a hydrocephalic fetus as any ethical fetal therapist would do, many elect not to have such fetal operations in light of the poor previous performances. This emphasizes how premature experimentation in the human situation can have unexpectedly disastrous consequences in influencing subsequent patient choice for a now improved therapy. This experience has highlighted the necessity of carefully controlled animal experiments before going into the human situation.

In experimental animals it has been possible to transplant kidneys, livers, and indeed hearts from one embryo or fetus into another. Indeed from a scientific and technical standpoint, such transplantations are easier than transplantations from embryos into adults or from adults into adults. This is because, for example, the embryo will grow to accommodate the extra tissue involved in a transplant, rejection problems are minimal, and one can restore function early in development and so avoid a number of disadvantageous secondary sequelae. Fetal to fetal transplantation in humans is therefore a possibility to correct for major structural abnormalities. As indicated previously, some, if not most, of these therapies will occur independent of *in vitro* fertilization, neither embryo having been conceived by this method. On the other hand it is possible that embryonic tissue derived from *in vitro* fertilizations, as outlined in the previous section, could be used for such fetal transplants.

The rate of progress in this field is quite phenomenal and can be judged by the fact that there have been two international congresses on fetal surgery and fetal medicine within the last year and there is now a dedicated specialist journal entitled *Fetal Therapy* devoted to publication of scientific and clinical articles in this area. It is very clear that manipulations of the embryo and fetus are likely to feature prominently in medical practice within the next ten years. They bring with them ethical problems which are different (but in some cases overlapping or complementary) to those of *in vitro* fertilization: such as, when is an embryo dead? What are the rights of donor or recipient embryos? What are the legal rights of an embryo or fetus as a patient? What is the relationship between the rights of the embryo and the rights of the mother when fetal intervention is clearly indicated but the mother refuses permission because of the attendant risks of maternal anaesthesia and surgery?

Experiments on animal embryos versus experiments on human embryos

Most investigators concerned with determining the mechanisms which control the development or maintenance or the pathogenesis of diseases in the adult would normally conduct experiments on animal models of these processes. Only when details had been elucidated in animals would experimenters turn to the human situation. I can think of no good reason why one would commence experiments on human embryos without first having investigated the phenomenon in animal embryos.

Nonetheless, once a certain body of knowledge has accumulated for animal embryos then one has to investigate the situation in humans. Essentially there are two choices here: either one conducts some very specifically defined experiments on human embryos, or one takes a risk and goes ahead with some kind of intervention based on knowledge gained in animal experiments but omitting the human investigative phase. Both approaches have their ethical problems. Certainly we know there are differences between early human embryos and early embryos from other mammals. Such differences include the stage of development at which the maternal genome remains active in the embryo, differences in the mechanisms of implantation, particularly cell surface molecules associated with this phenomenon, and differences in spatial organization and gene expression. Clearly there are a whole host of areas where we have no idea whether there are major differences between experimental animals and humans because the situation has not been investigated in the latter. Some form of experimentation on early human embryos to determine specific mechanisms, having first investigated the phenomenon in animals, would appear a rational approach, probably more rational than some current approaches which omit the human experimentation phase and essentially begin with therapeutic experimentations on either embryos or adults.

Paradoxically embryos which develop abnormally from an *in vitro* fertilization programme could be the ones of greatest interest. To exemplify this, consider the following scenario. Supposing an embryo was produced by *in vitro* fertilization and divided so that it had a genetically identical clone which was frozen; one embryo was reimplanted and developed abnormally with some major defect. One would then know that the frozen embryo would be likely to develop the same defect and so one would be able to investigate mechanisms causing this disorder at very early stages when it would normally be impossible to know whether the disorder was going to develop. This theoretical possibility has been put forward by individuals wishing to create a scare about *in vitro* fertilization. It is true that it represents a rational approach to a disease problem and it is equally true that one could generate useful data from this approach. However, it is likely that such incidences will be rare and therefore the natural opportunities for conducting such experimentation extraordinarily limited. It is this very limitation which makes the approach unfeasible from the scientific perspective. In order to investigate the mechanisms of most disease processes thoroughly, a large number of embryos would be required and these would clearly not be generated by the scenario above. Whilst the scenario outlined remains a theoretical possibility and could be utilized in individual cases, I must again emphasize that it is likely to be extraordinarily rare.

It is also very important not to overplay the value of experimentation on early human embryos as against experimentation utilizing cells or tissues derived from older embryos or adults, or utilizing animal models. Much has been said about the role of early embryos generated by *in vitro* fertilization procedures in investigations such as the mechanisms of causation of cancer. Such mechanisms are highly complex and I would find it difficult to make a case for any particular disorder requiring exclusively experimentation on early human embryos. It is true that one might utilize cells derived from early human embryos in the course of investigations which have earlier utilized animal models or cells derived from adults. It would however be easy to overplay the use of early embryonic tissue to a degree where it became a scientific nonsense.

Fictional scenarios – big on sensation but low on scientific credibility

Cloning

Cloning is a word greatly misused in the popular press. Essentially there are two types of cloning. One is the cloning of a cell or a cell line. Quite simply this means that a single cell, whether from an embryo or from an adult, is selected and grown under special culture conditions in isolation so that it divides many times. The progeny of this cell are said to be cloned, i.e. they are all derived from the same individual cell. Cellular cloning has little relevance to ethical considerations of *in vitro* fertilization or embryo manipulation.

Cloning of embryos is another matter. It is possible to divide the early mammalian embryo into two and possibly into four separate viable embryos. Such divisions can occur naturally and result in identical or monozygotic twins or quadruplets. However, it is impossible to keep dividing the early mammalian embryo to produce more and more identical offspring. Development in the early embryo is programmed, and blastocoel formation (i.e. formation of the cavity within the early developing embryo) occurs after a preprogrammed number of divisions regardless of the cell number or mass in the embryo. Should the cell number fall below a critical threshold, the mass develops into a non-viable trophoblast lacking any inner cell mass and hence any embryo. Therefore unlimited cloning by embryonic division is impossible; at best quadruplets might be produced.

The other approach to cloning involves removing the nuclei from cells of the early embryo and replacing them with nuclei from either other embryonic cells or adult cells. This procedure of nuclear removal and transplantation is extraordinarily difficult to perform, particularly between adult and embryonic cells.

Even if such procedures were applied to embryos developed from *in vitro* fertilization programmes, they would not result in an individual who was identical either to the individual from whom the nucleus was removed, or to the one developed individual from the four embryo clones generated by embryonic division.

The reason is simple. First, the cytoplasm plays some role in directing gene expression and so cells created by nuclear transplantation are never identical to the donor because of this cytoplasmic difference. Moreover, the embryonic environment *in utero*, including the volume and composition of the amniotic fluid, the state of nutrition, the state of maternal health, ingested compounds, etc., have large influences on embryonic development. Consequently, four genetically identical embryos allowed to develop in the same mother at different times would not turn out to be identical. Environmental influences would come into play. Moreoever, the co-ordination and local regulation of embryonic development depend on epigenetic and environmental influences and these would also ensure that the embryos were not the same. It is true to say, however, that they would be remarkably similar but for them to be truly identical these embryos would all have to develop in the same mother at the same time under identical *in utero* conditions. They would also have to be reared in postnatal life under fairly identical conditions. All of this is very implausible.

Therefore the possibility of indefinitely cloning individuals, or the scenario of the mad rich dictator who wishes to populate the world with identical copies of himself are pure fiction from a scientific standpoint.

Cloning has been suggested as a way of providing a reservoir of antigenically identical spare parts for later life. As explained earlier in this chapter, it would appear that research into the control of antigenic determinants on embryonic cells would render this complex procedure unnecessary from a therapeutic standpoint. Moreover, there are indications that division of the early embryo into two or into four separate parts may not be without some minor penalty in later development.

I believe that arguments put forward on the basis of cloning are pure fiction. Moreover, as I indicated earlier, the time span between manipulation and effect is very long in the human population, much longer than any dictator or megalomaniac would be able to sustain. If one really wanted to control human behaviour or some other parameter on a mass population scale, then one would be better off doing it by chemical additives to the water supply rather than by genetic manipulation of early embryos!

Human-animal hybrids

It has been suggested that *in vitro* fertilization techniques could be used to cross human gametes with those from other species. This is currently technically impossible, and is likely to remain so. In order to fertilize an egg of one species with a sperm from a different species, the outer covering of the oocyte must be removed; once this is removed the oocyte, even when fertilized, rapidly loses viability. Moreoever, the uterus of any animal has a complex immunological relationship with the embryo which facilitates implantation and successful pregnancy. It is unlikely that either of these could occur with a human-animal hybrid: the conceptus would almost certainly be rejected. Worries about such human-animal hybrids have probably arisen from hamster tests to investigate human sperm fusion and sperm head decondensation in subfertile human males. Using this technique, hamster eggs are fertilized by human sperm, and the assay is a useful one. However, the fertilized egg rapidly dies after a small number of cell divisions. Other fears may have arisen from early experiments which attempted (unsuccessfully) to culture human embryos in the fallopian tubes of other animals such as sheep and rabbits. The objective of such experiments was to create an environment for early human development which mimicked that present normally. This environment is now provided by *in vitro* culture conditions but the early experiments attest to the fact that human-animal hybrids are unlikely to be a real possibility.

Ectogenesis or full development outside the human body

One fictional scenario put forward as a worry of *in vitro* fertilization is that it would be possible to grow embryos all the way through gestation outside the womb. At present this is not achievable in any animal and indeed the problems are so complex that the future holds little hope of complete ectogenesis. The environment of fetal development within the mother is highly complex in terms of nutrition, growth factors, endocrinological control, osmotic buffering, etc., and it would be extraordinarily difficult to replicate all of these conditions *in vitro*. For the foreseeable future I believe that ectogenesis is impossible. It is also sobering for those who are worried about the impact of molecular biology on the course of human development to consider that the development of an artificial womb will probably have little to do with molecular biology and more to do with conventional physiology, endocrinology and cell biology.

Male mothers

Another fictional scenario often put forward for *in vitro* fertilization is that appropriate hormonal treatment of males could result in *in vitro* fertilized embryos being implanted and developing normally in the male. Once again the complex anatomical, physiological, and endocrinological events surrounding pregnancy make it almost impossible that these could be replicated in the male. So from a scientific standpoint I also view this possibility as complete fiction.

Brain transplantation

Various fictional scenarios have been proposed in which clones of individual embryos or even adults with deliberate brain damage are kept alive for use as biological spare parts. Other scenarios paint the picture of complete brain transplants from either one embryo into another or embryos into adults or even adults into adults. The complex connections both within the central nervous system and from the central nervous system to the peripheral nervous system make any kind of large-scale brain transplantation next to impossible. It is certainly true that very small segments of the brain may be transplanted, e.g. cells may be placed in a particular area to restore function which has been lost through disease or trauma or ageing. However, complete brain transplants to change an individual's personality or intelligence are pure fiction from a scientific standpoint.

In this chapter I have attempted to put forward some of the contemporary and future possibilities for manipulating early human development. In reviewing a large body of previously published material on this topic, mostly in articles dealing with ethics, the following points became abundantly clear. First, it is important for scientists realistically to state what is scientifically possible both at an individual and at a population level. Second, it is important that scientists do not exaggerate either the extent of such manipulations or their possible advantages. Third, it is important that those who for one reason or another may oppose *in vitro* fertilization and early embryonic manipulation do not either exaggerate or invent future possibilities which have little resemblance to scientific fact.

I feel certain that there are future possibilities which I have not highlighted in this chapter and which may become evident at any time. As with all progress, there will always be groups who extol or condemn the advances being made. Only by examining the objective data and its implications both at the individual family, and population level can one hope to have a balanced discussion on the ethics of the procedures. Only by such measures can society hope to pursue a path of rationality in the application of such advances.

Notes

1 Totipotential cells are cells capable of becoming any cell within the body.
2 Teratocarcinomas are tumours whose development mirrors many of the biological events occurring during embryonic development.
3 The protein which is involved in the cascade of protein interactions which allows blood to clot.

Further reading

Basic Molecular and Cellular Biology. A series of articles which appeared in the *British Medical Journal*, published in book format by the British Medical Journal, 1988.

Cherfas, J. (1982) *Manmade Life*, Oxford: Basil Blackwell.

Edwards, R. G., and Purdy, J. (1981) *Human Conception* In Vitro, London: Academic Press.

Ferguson, M. W. J. (1989) 'Dentistry and the new biology', *British Dental Journal*.

Fishel, S., and Symonds, E. M. (1986) In Vitro *Fertilization. Past, Present, Future*, Oxford: IRL Press.

Harris, J. (1983) '*In vitro* fertilisation: the ethical issues', *The Philosophical Quarterly* 33.132, 217–37.

Hogan, B., Constantini, F., Lacy, E. (1986) *Manipulating the Mouse Embryo. A Laboratory Manual*, Cold Spring Harbor Laboratory, USA.

MacLeod, A., and Sikora, K. (1984) *Molecular Biology and Human Disease*, Oxford: Blackwell Scientific Publications.

Monk, M. (1987) *Mammalian Development. A Practical Approach*, Oxford: IRL Press.

Nossal, G. L. V. (1984) *Reshaping Life. Key Issues in Genetic Engineering*, Melbourne: Melbourne University Press.

Palmiter, R. D., and Brinster, R. L. (1986) *Annual Review of Genetics* 20, 465–565.

Seppala, M., and Edwards, R. G. (1985) '*In vitro* fertilisation and embryo transfer', *Annals of the New York Academy of Sciences* 442.

Weatherall, D. J. (1985) *The New Genetics and Clinical Practice*, 2nd edition, Oxford: Oxford University Press.

Chapter two

Historical perspectives on human embryo research

Edward Yoxen

The purpose of this chapter is to argue that the viewing of present concern about human embryo research in historical perspective has some value. From the intensity of recent debate we might suppose that it is only with the appearance and expansion of procedures for the *in vitro* fertilization of human ova in the 1970s and 1980s that morally significant actions involving human embryos have occurred. Thus we might say that it is not only unsurprising but also appropriate that such research should have attracted such attention in the past three to four years, as disquiet has spread amongst sections of the public, and within the medical, legal, and religious professions, about a rapidly expanding practice. However, I believe this is in two ways a distorted reading of events.

First, it is not the case that morally significant actions relating to human embryos originated with *in vitro* fertilization. Rather, different research procedures (involving thousands of human embryos and fetuses assembled into collections of specimens) have been followed for at least a hundred years, which raise serious moral questions. We should at least note this fact in assessing the apparent novelty of what is happening now. This is not to say that there are no new dimensions, but that the recurring issues may well be the more important.

Second, the mere expansion in scale of a procedure and the increased publicity given to it do not in themselves explain public comment and opposition. Nor do they alone indicate why a particular prioritization of the moral issues should have taken place.

A common theme in recent debates about what may legitimately be done with human embryos has been the notion of their intrinsic rights, which renders various experimental and storage procedures unacceptable. This forces one to ask why this formulation is being deployed now, and why this kind of appeal is being made. My own view, argued elsewhere and not developed here, is that explanations of present concern should be sought through changes in the political climate in Britain and through the related shifts in moral sensibility.[1] For instance, there are other ways in which moral questions relating to human embryos could be posed. Since such embryos are only available to science through the co-operation of women, either by the ending of a pregnancy or by the removal of ova prior to fertilization, we could certainly say that their rights to uncompromised medical care and their feelings about the use of something that was once (or would have been) part of them, are primary. Yet the prioritization of the alleged rights of the human embryo distracts attention from this question. It is easy to draw the provisional conclusion, although much more work is needed to substantiate it fully, that present concern about human embryos serves to undermine, and in certain quarters at least is consciously *intended* to undermine, some of the political and cultural advantages that women have won in recent years, by devaluing and marginalizing women's reproductive experience.[2]

Amongst other things this also prompts the question of whether there has been concern in the past about activities with human embryos and, if so, whether such concern has functioned in a similar fashion. I am not in a position to tackle this question here. Indeed all I seek to do is to make the point that present activities can usefully be seen as part of a tradition of investigations which goes back at least a hundred years, if not for two millenia, and to point out that the use of human embryos in medical research has not suddenly become morally significant through the innovation of *in vitro* fertilization. This is a useful point at which to make the comment that I am of course here referring to human embryos and fetuses from various states of development, and that I tend to use the former term throughout, when fetus would be conventional. But in one sense this is scarcely relevant in that, despite their developmental differences, what they all have in common is that they arise from the germinal material of women, and until the late 1960s could only be obtained by removal, or after loss, from women's bodies. Moreover by the 1940s already human embryos of only 7½ days old were the subject of research. It is not as if only fetal research took place until human *in vitro* fertilization was achieved.

In 1931 the Cambridge biochemist, Joseph Needham, published his monograph *Chemical Embryology*, of which the first four chapters formed a detailed treatment of the history of the subject, up to the end of the eighteenth century. Three years later they appeared as *A History of Embryology*.[3] This is a work of remarkable erudition, with over a thousand sources in English, French, German, Italian, and Latin cited in the fifty-page bibliography. It also shows great sensitivity to historical context. Although Needham was a working scientist at this time, just beginning his study of embryonic induction using chick and amphibian embryos, it is not an account of science as steadily accumulating truths, or of mistakes cast aside by the work of geniuses. A recurrent theme is the operation of limiting factors – cultural, institutional, technical, conceptual, and methodological – that inhibit inquiry at any moment in time. Thus, for example, scientists may be unable to conceive a particular problem or to make any headway with it because they lack the necessary ideas with which to plan experiments and interpret the results. Whilst this had been true in the past – of William Harvey in the seventeenth century, for example – Needham believed this was also true of the 1930s, when 'the most urgent need of modern embryology is a series of advances of a purely theoretical, even mathematico-logical nature.'[4] With other Cambridge colleagues he was a member of the so-called Theoretical Biology Club throughout the decade, and came close to founding an institute along these lines, before turning away from experimental science for good in the 1940s, to begin his now classic encyclopaedic studies of the history of Chinese science.[5] As an embryologist Needham exemplified that heuristic and inspirational interest in the history of science common in that discipline even today.[6]

In 1944 the American biologist George Corner gave the Terry Lectures at Yale University, endowed to build '... the truths of science and philosophy into the structure of a broadened and purified religion'.[7] These three lectures appeared in the same year as *Ourselves Unborn: An Embryologist's Essay on Man*. Corner's purpose was to describe and meditate upon recent work on embryogenesis, on hereditary malformation and on phylogenetic similarities between embryos of different species. It is a much shorter book than Needham's; the style is less ponderous and the historical scope is far less ambitious. But it too is an attempt to use the experimental findings of embryologists as a cultural resource, to call into question religious and moral doctrines about the beginning of life, to demolish certain popular ideas about the vulnerability of the fetus to maternal experiences, and to stress both the evolutionary continuity of the human species with the rest of living nature and its uniqueness. Each chapter beings with an apt biblical quotation. Corner clearly intended it as a scientist's act of devotion.

Taken together, these two books provide an interesting way of viewing human embryology in historical perspective as it appeared in the 1930s and 1940s. Thus Needham, writing about investigations in a whole range of species, shows the enormously long history of attempts to explain the everyday phenomena of mating, gestation, growth of a fetus, birth, and generational similarity, using scientific concepts such as germinal material, preformation, and hereditary determinant. But he has little to say about human embryology as such, principally because of the difficulty until the late nineteenth century of making specific comments. His volume closes around 1800, before the remarkable expansion of experimental embryology, assisted by the cell theory of Schleiden and Schwann.[8] A successor volume was never written. He describes embryological endeavours as part of zoological inquiry, or even more generally as natural philosophy, in which investigators struggled against the limits of experimental technique and existing theory, often without fully realizing how these limits functioned. That sense of not knowing why certain methodologies, which are highly successful in other areas, but which seem to break down in studies of development, persists in much embryology today.

Corner, on the other hand, focuses almost entirely on late nineteenth and early twentieth century investigations, basing his remarks largely on detailed anatomical and histological studies of human embryos, preserved in collections around the world, including the very few of just over seven days old available in the 1940s. Virtually all the work cited is closely linked with clinical practice, by being based on material taken from patients and oriented to an understanding of human development and its pathology.

Two different modes of embryological research are involved here. Needham's scientists usually perform dissections of whole animals and occasionally human fetuses, and are concerned with rather general theoretical questions: What is the nature of the fertilization process? What is the role of the germinal material of either sex? Is embryological development the realization of a pre-formed being? In what form does the embryo enter the uterus? Corner's embryologists on the other hand collect, section, draw, stain and analyse human embryos obtained from miscarriages or from surgical intervention in pregnancy, and tend to be concerned with more specific questions: How do particular developmental abnormalities arise? To what extent are embryos of different species similar? At what stage does the embryo of a particular species become implanted in the uterine wall?

For the purposes of this chapter it must be sufficient simply to note the existence of a very long tradition of both theoretical and empirical inquiry concerning embryological development. Needham, in typically encyclopaedic style, refers to magical beliefs about fetuses in many primitive cultures which also appear in the European alchemical tradition and in cabbalistic writings, and to the extensive discussion of embryology in early Chinese and Indian natural philosophy and medical theory, *before* describing the ideas of Greek biologists like Aristotle and Galen, which retained their influence until at least the sixteenth century.[9] As one might expect of a Marxist of this generation, Needham is keen to explore the possible links between commitment to particular theories and social class, but ignores the sexual asymmetry in both Aristotelian and Galenic writings. Indeed he applauds the takeover of obstetrics from allegedly unskilled midwives by physician-scientists as making more embryological investigation possible. Such issues are treated very differently today.[10]

The early Middle Ages saw an important reawakening of theoretical interest in procreation and development, prior to the more empirical anatomical studies of Renaissance anatomists like Fabricius and Fallopius. Such were the conventions of natural philosophical discourse at the time that a discussion of ensoulment might be thought entirely relevant to what we would now take to be a discussion of inertial motion.[11]

By the seventeenth century investigators such as William Harvey, physician to Charles I, were able to pose much more precise questions about the development of the early embryo in order to test particular theories of generation and development. If, as Aristotle had suggested, the embryo was formed through the interaction of menstrual blood and semen in the uterus as a result of copulation, it should be possible to locate the embryo in the uterus very soon afterwards. If it could not be found, then presumably this theory of germinal fusion was wrong, and one might argue, as Harvey did, that the formation of embryos occurred through some sort of non-material influence of the male semen that eventually caused the appearance of a fertilized egg in the uterus.

Harvey, a committed Aristotelian, pursued these ideas in studies of the king's deer herd, with the active interest of the monarch and his court circle. Individual does were killed at different intervals after mating and the uterine contents examined. To his great puzzlement he failed to locate embryos in the uterus for a long while after copulation, in effect undermining Aristotelian doctrine. Harvey's great authority as a medical scientist stimulated considerable interest in understanding fertilization and development. Later in the century the Dutch scientist Regnier de Graaf discovered that the ovaries of mammals had a characteristic fine structure, now described by the term 'follicles', which he wrongly identified as eggs. This led to much consideration of preformationist theories of embryonic development in the early eighteenth century.[12] Moreover the Harveian belief persisted, promoted by such commanding figures as Albrecht von Haller, that the decisive modification of the ovum occurred in the uterus, rather than *en route* through the oviduct.[13]

At the same time the rehabilitation of atomism in the seventeenth century, and its productive use in physics and chemistry, led some scientists to contemplate its application to the processes of change characteristic of growth and development. Thus for a fetus to acquire a changing form, to enlarge in size, and to develop internal organs, matter must be transformed, organized, distributed, and built into definite structures – into tissue, into organs, and into whole organisms maintained in existence through the functioning of physiological systems. Whereas Aristotelian natural philosphers held that it was adequate to speak of such phenomena as arising through the impression of form on unformed matter, since the seventeenth century it has been scientifically conventional to regard such statements as question-begging. But, at the same time, if we are to think of living organisms as composed of particulate matter subject to countless mechanical interactions, then how are we to understand the genesis of phenomena characteristic of living things, such as apparently purposive behaviour, volition (in human beings as least), and development? This is an important theme in eighteenth century scientific debates, in the aftermath of the successes of atomism in physics, between the proponents of different kinds of materialism on the one hand and vitalists, animists, and idealists on the other. By the early nineteenth century this debate is complicated by the strengthening view that the organization of living matter has a history, that its different forms have been subject to evolution.[14]

Against this background of constantly shifting debate about the adequacy of explanatory frameworks in the life-sciences, invest-igations in embryology continued. In 1827 the Estonian scientist, Karl Ernst von Baer, demonstrated through the sacrifice of a friend's bitch in heat that ovulation in mammals leads to the appearance of a mature egg in a fluid-filled sac on the surface of the ovary.[15] It must therefore travel along the oviduct to be fertilized and later to implant in the wall of the uterus. It was a hundred years before similar evidence was available for human ovulation.[16] Much nineteenth century embryology was devoted to investigating the processes by which embryos organize and reorganize themselves in development. Are there, for example, basic structural transformations that are common to all embryos? Investigators like Bischoff and Remak claimed that there were, with three different kinds of tissue being distinguishable, each with a different role to play later in develop-ment. By mid-century the idea of performing experiments with mammalian embryos, to test hypotheses about such developmental mechanisms, had taken root.

Experimentation in this fashion was limited to particular species, such as rabbits, from which early embryos could be removed prior to implantation. In the 1880s the Cambridge physiologist, Walter Heape, succeeded in transferring rabbit embryos from one animal to another on the point of a needle, in order to demonstrate both that implantation and gestation in another animal was possible and that there were no lasting effects on a superior female animal of mating with an inferior male.[17] In other words the uterus only functioned as a nurturative environment; it did not receive 'hereditary impressions' from the embryo as it were, which would then be passed on to subsequent offspring. This contradicted a widely held belief in animal breeding. Heape was an early member of a school of reproductive physiologists in Cambridge who pioneered the study of how the class of physiologically active substances known as 'hormones' acted to regulate physiological processes, such as ovulation, implantation, gestation, and delivery. Much of this work by Hammond, Parkes, Austin, and others, was done on agricultural animals, but important connections were established with medical researchers working on human reproductive cycles, of whom George Corner, the discoverer of progesterone, was one.[18]

However, the important point at this stage is to note that, although experimental embryology expanded significantly in the second half of the nineteenth century with dissections and investigations of animal and amphibian embryos, and although slightly later work in reproductive physiology threw light on ovulation and gestation, work on human embryos was necessarily limited to the dissection of dead or dying specimens obtained in hospital. It was in effect an extension of comparative anatomy. The kinds of general theoretical question about which Joseph Needham was writing were not easily accessible in this way. Instead human embryologists were limited to the establishment of a 'database', in the form of collections of human embryos at various stages of development, and the inductive construction of tables of developmental stages, indicating norms of growth and the process of complexification for particular periods of gestation. Since congenital abnormality had been recognized for millenia, although its causes were widely debated, and since some human embryos showed developmental abnormality to occur very early on, some investigators began to ask themselves how and what kinds of disruptions of development could lead to such anatomical changes.

Thus in 1913 Franklin P. Mall, Professor of Anatomy at Johns Hopkins University in Baltimore, an important centre of the scientific modernization of medicine, published 'A plea for an Institute of Human Embryology' in the *Journal of the American Medical Association*.[19] In it he refers to the Naples Zoological Station in Italy, at that time an important example of the value of

33

experimental investigation in the life sciences, and to the plans of the German anatomist, Wilhelm His, with whom Mall had trained. His had promoted various systematizing, collaborative studies, based on preserved human embryos, and Mall had himself built up such a collection.

> The collection in Baltimore includes five hundred specimens which have been accumulated during a period of twenty years. It contains about one hundred normal embryos cut into serial sections, of which about one fifth are really good specimens ranging from 2 to 30 mm in length. Although great care has been taken to collect good histories of these specimens, they are still fragmentary, and by no means as reliable and extensive as they should be. Since, however, the quality of the specimens and histories is gradually improving, there is every assurance that a much better collection could be obtained under more favourable conditions. This collection is the result of the efforts of one individual largely unaided. The Leipsic collection was also made by a single individual during a period of thirty-five years. In scientific value it is probably inferior to the Baltimore collection for it antedates it. Since the death of His the collection has fallen out of use; in fact, most investigators do not know what has become of it. The other collections, which are smaller and scattered, have been drawn on freely by Keibel for his Normentafeln and by Keibel and Mall for the *Manual of Human Embryology*. This is our present state.[20]

Mall goes on to stress the organizational and scientific advantages that would flow from the creation of a modern research institute, based around a collection of embryos.

> With a very large collection, a competent staff and the very best material equipment the institute would naturally take up problems which bear on anatomy, physical anthropology, comparative embryology, physiology of gestation, pathology and teratology. The following larger questions suggest themselves:
>
> 1 Curve of growth.
> 2 Anatomy of various stages.
> 3 Morphology of the brain.
> 4 Histogenesis.
> 5 Cause of abortion.
> 6 Study of monsters.
> 7 Study of moles.
> 8 Comparative and experimental embryology to elucidate human.[21]

In the event Mall's plea was answered by the Carnegie Institution and by an institute established in Baltimore. There the largest collection of human embryos in the world was assembled and a famous monograph series was published annually, in what became an important centre of research on several fronts.[22] Mall was its first director. After him came George Streeter, who was succeeded in turn by George Corner until 1956. In 1971 the entire collection was transferred to the Medical School of the University of California at Davis.[23] Thus whilst Needham could plan a programme of general embryological research, based in one of the pre-eminent bio-chemistry departments in the world established by Frederick Gowland Hopkins, with a major historical survey, Corner could draw upon unrivalled archival and technical resources in human embryology to develop his interests in the interactions between the physiology of reproductive hormone secretion, uterine function, and human development.

His, Mall, Corner, and others were in effect systematizing and centralizing a practice that had been current amongst doctors for some while, namely of collecting interesting embryonic specimens for their own use. Indeed, they were often referred to, like papyri, by the name of their current owner. Their sections were reproduced in textbooks and their salient features argued over in journal articles. By any standards this is research. Whilst one could exaggerate the moral or symbolic significance of their having become available through the trauma of miscarriage, major surgery, or death in pregnancy, it is striking that in professional discourse this is treated as an irrelevance. It would be interesting to know for example whether this professional appropriation of once-living material was ever contested.

Elsewhere in America other physicians and researchers were pursuing interests which raise related moral questions rather more sharply. In Boston from the early years of this century the obstetrician John Rock pursued a long-standing interest in infertility through studies of the changing condition of the endometrium, the tissue lining the uterus, through the menstrual cycle. His sometime collaborator, the Harvard pathologist Arthur Hertig, took up investigations of embryonic and uterine abnormalities. In Worcester, Massachusetts, the physiologist Gregory Pincus, who had worked in Cambridge, England, with Hammond and Parkes on animal studies, concerned himself with the maturation of ova prior to ovulation, and its hormonal regulation.[24]

By the end of the 1930s Rock and Hertig were searching for fertilized human ova in the Fallopian tubes and uteruses removed from women who had sought sterilization from Rock. Their operations were timed to be slightly later than their estimated date of ovulation, in the hope that they might have had intercourse before coming into hospital and, unbeknown to them, have conceived. In a very small number of cases this was indeed so, and from their organs Hertig removed both fertilized and unfertilized ova, which were then sectioned, examined and made part of the Baltimore collection. In fact one of the plates in Corner's book of 1944 was produced in just this way.[25] Whilst the women concerned had consented to surgery, it is not clear whether they were aware that Rock and Hertig were searching for human embryos. According to Rock's biographer, Loretta McLaughlin, Rock and Hertig did not instruct women to engage in intercourse prior to surgery but only to record the dates when they had done so. However their erstwhile assistant, Miriam Menkin, admitted that she did indeed do so, to increase the chances of obtaining an embryo.[26] Furthermore the operations were delayed for several months whilst the women returned to the hospital as charity patients bearing temperature charts, from which the date for surgery was computed.

This work led to an interest in *in vitro* fertilization. In 1937 an unsigned editorial appeared in the *New England Journal of Medicine* suggesting that recent work by Rock and Pincus might lead to a new way of alleviating the involuntary infertility caused by blocked Fallopian tubes.[27] It is thought that Rock was in fact the author of this article. In any event by the early 1940s he and his assistant Miriam Menkin were attempting to fertilize human tubal ova, obtained from Rock's hysterectomy patients, using semen from Rock's junior doctors. In 1944 they believed that they had succeeded and published a paper in *Science* which made this claim.[28] This now seems very unlikely for technical reasons. Whatever its actual technical status, this work received considerable public comment, complicated and perhaps intensified by the fact that John Rock, a prominent and well-known figure in Boston society, was also a devout Roman Catholic. As one would expect, this manipulation of human germ cells was condemned as immoral by the prelates of his Church, and the local and national press commented at length on the morality of this achievement and its possible implications. Amongst other things, when its possible role in dealing with infertility became clear, Rock received letters from women asking for assistance in this way. However, this possibility was not taken up and Rock soon changed his research interests, to something at least as controversial, namely the development of an oral contraceptive pill, with Gregory Pincus. Hertig, on the other hand, continued to collect early human embryos, and in 1959 published a paper on 34 of them, obtained from 210 women, as a study in human reproductive success.[29]

Several other scientists published similar claims of *in vitro* fertilization with both human and animal ova through the 1950s. An authoritative review in 1957 dismissed all these claims as most likely to be mistaken.[30] However in 1959 Chang published a paper describing an experiment with well-designed genetic controls, which demonstrated that *in vitro* fertilization of mouse eggs was possible. It was of course a further ten years before Edwards, Steptoe, and Bavister made similar claims for human ova, although their conclusions of their paper in *Nature* were immediately queried by the Cambridge zoologist, Lord Victor Rothschild.[31] The following year they published another paper in which they produced evidence of development to the blastocyst stage after *in vitro* fertilization of human ova, which was much harder to question. However, Edwards and his colleagues could also claim to have viewed live human embryos for the first time. As Edwards has recounted in *A Matter of Life*, from the early 1970s he and Steptoe were engaged in a programme of research to test the safety of their procedures, by searching for chromosomal abnormalities in embryos created in this way, in order to prepare for its utilization as a clinical procedure, as the 1937 editorial had suggested.[32]

These papers attracted very considerable public comment, much of it critical in various ways. Some scientists were impelled to move into the field themselves, notably Soupart and Howard Jones in the US, Carl Wood in Australia, and Jacques Testart in France. In America however the researchers soon discovered that the climate of public opinion, in the wake of the controversial Supreme Court Roe *v.* Wade decision in 1973, which had liberalized abortion law to a significant extent, was not at all conducive to experimentation in this area. It became clear, for example, that public funds from the National Institutes of Health would not be forthcoming, and that researchers could expect vigorous local opposition from anti-abortion groups, concerned that research on 'the unborn', however conceived, should not flourish.[33]

In the United Kingdom the situation was somewhat different. The major change in abortion law took place a little earlier, in 1967. A very rapid increase in the numbers of abortions being performed resulted, so that an inquiry into the workings of the Act was set up in 1970. Similarly there was some concern that research on aborted human fetuses was taking place in an unregulated fashion. However, anti-abortion groups did not have the political leverage to bring about a moratorium on human embryo research at that time, as they had done in effect in the United States. A committee under the chairmanship of Sir John Peel was asked to draw up guidelines for fetal research. This report appeared in 1972.[34] Its concern is exclusively with the moral status of experiments done on dead and dying fetuses obtained either by surgical abortion or by spontaneous miscarriage, and on experiments on fetuses in the womb whose existence is to be ended by imminent abortion. The committee drew up guidelines and limits which remain the basis of medical research policy in this area today. Interestingly, however, they did not consider experimentation with human embryos, although clearly they could have done so. Moreover parliamentary and governmental interest in *in vitro* fertilization and related research has come later in the UK than in several other countries, notably the US and Australia.

Following the Peel report the Medical Research Council, foreseeing that the use of fetal tissue would be of enduring interest to researchers in many fields, and would also be likely to remain a controversial area politically, set up a central facility to store such material at the Royal Marsden Hospital, so as to be able to claim that all experiments using fetal material were subject to a degree of central scrutiny.[35] However, as the recent concern with fetal tissue transplants indicates, some such material can circulate locally in the hospital system.

The use of human embryos created by *in vitro* fertilization for a variety of research purposes has expanded considerably with the diffusion of *in vitro* fertilization as a medical procedure. The development of techniques for freezing embryos through the 1950s and 1960s has considerably increased the possibilities for research, since embryos can be stored. Moreover the frequent use of hormones that induce superovulation has increased the supply of surplus ova within *in vitro* fertilization programmes. Despite that, some researchers have chosen to modernize and modify the strategy followed by Rock, Menkin, and Hertig in the 1940s, by asking women seeking hysterectomies to undergo superovulation so as to allow ova to be removed from their ovaries for subsequent *in vitro* fertilization.[36] The resulting embryos are either donated to women seeking to become pregnant or, more usually, used for research. Regrettably, there is already anecdotal evidence that women are offered operations much sooner if they will agree to act as donors. In my view this simply underlines the historical conclusion that in evaluating human embryo research we should attend primarily to the rights and feelings of the women who would make it possible, rather than to the characteristics of the potentiated cluster of cells we call an embryo, even though in the past this has not happened.

Notes

1 This issue is considered in E. J. Yoxen, 'Social concern, legislation and policy: the case of human embryo research in Britain in the 1980s', to appear in M. McNeil *et al.* (eds), *Social Dimensions of the New Reproductive Technologies* (London: Macmillan, forthcoming); see also E. J. Yoxen, *Public Concern and the Steering of Science* (London: Science Policy Support Group, Concept Paper No. 7, 1988).

2 This point is made in M. Stanworth, 'Reproductive technologies and the deconstruction of motherhood' in M. Stanworth (ed.), *Reproductive Technologies: Gender, Motherhood and Medicine* (Cambridge: Polity Press, 1987), 10–35.

3 J. Needham, *A History of Embryology* (Cambridge: Cambridge University Press, 1934: second edition, 1959). References are to the second edition.

4 Ibid, p. 240.

5 Much biographical information about Needham is to be found in P. G. Werskey, *The Visible College* (London: Allen Lane, 1978); see also the Festschrift to Needham, which contains a pseudonymous, autobiographical essay, M. Teich, R. M. Young (eds), *Changing Perspectives in the History of Science: Essays in Honour of Joseph Needham* (London: Heinemann, 1973); see also D. J. Haraway, *Crystals, Fabrics and Fields: Metaphors of Organicism in Twentieth Century Developmental Biology* (London: Yale University Press, 1976).

6 The outstanding example is T. J. Horder *et al.*, *A History of Embryology* (Cambridge: Cambridge University Press, 1986).

7 G. W. Corner, *Ourselves Unborn: An Embryologist's Essay on Man* (New Haven: Yale University Press, 1944).

8 C. W. Bodemer, 'The biology of the blastocyst in historical perspective' in R. J. Blandau (ed.), *The Biology of the Blastocyst* (London: University of Chicago Press, 1971), 1–25; see also W. Coleman, *Biology in the Nineteenth Century: Problems of Form, Function and Transformation* (New York: Wiley, 1971).

9 A. Preus, 'Science and philosophy in Aristotle's *Generation of Animals*', *Journal of the History of Biology* 3 (1970), 1–52; M. C. Horowitz, 'Aristotle and women', ibid, 9 (1976), 186–213; M. Boylan, 'Galen's conception theory', ibid, 19 (1986), 47–78.

10 See for example A. McLaren, *Reproductive Rituals: The Perception of Fertility in England from the Sixteenth to the Nineteenth Century* (London: Methuen, 1984).

11 E. J. Dijksterhuis, *The Mechanization of the World Picture* (Oxford: Clarendon Press, 1961).

12 S. A. Roe, *Matter, Life and Generation: 18th Century Embryology and the Haller-Wolff Debate* (Cambridge: Cambridge University Press, 1981).

13 See Bodemer, op. cit. (see note 8 above).

14 A. O. Lovejoy, *The Great Chain of Being: A Study of the History of an Idea* (New York: Harper, 1960).

15 G. Sarton, 'The discovery of the mammalian egg and the foundation of

modern embryology', *Isis* 16 (1931), 315–30.

16 E. Allen *et al.*, 'Recovery of human ova from the uterine tubes: time of ovulation in the menstrual cycle', *Journal of the Americal Medical Association* 91 (1928), 1018–20; see also K. J. Betteridge, 'An historical look at embryo transfer', *Journal of Reproduction and Fertility* 62 (1981), 1–13.

17 W. Heape, 'Preliminary note on the transplantation and growth of mammalian ova within a uterine foster-mother', *Proceedings of the Royal Society* 48 (1891), 457–8; idem, 'Further note on ...', ibid, 62 (1897–8), 178–83.

18 M. Borrell, 'Organotherapy and reproductive physiology', *Journal of the History of Biology* 18 (1985), 1–30.

19 F. P. Mall, 'A plea for an institute of human embryology', *Journal of the Americal Medical Association* 60.21 (May 24 1913), 1599–1601.

20 Ibid, p. 1600.

21 Ibid, p. 1601.

22 The monograph series was entitled *Contributions to Embryology* and appeared annually.

23 D. D. Brown, 'The Department of Embryology of the Carnegie Institution of Washington', *BioEssays* 6.2 (1987), 92–6.

24 L. McLaughlin, *The Pill, John Rock and the Church: The Biography of a Revolution* (Boston: Little, Brown, 1982); on Pincus see P. J. Pauly, *Controlling Life: Jacques Loeb and the Engineering Ideal in Biology* (New York: Oxford University Press, 1987), Chapter 8.

25 This forms Plate III facing page 18 in Corner's book. The embryo is referred to as Carnegie Collection No. 8020.

26 McLaughlin, op. cit. (see note 24 above), p. 75: for a discussion of this work see G. Corea, *The Mother Machine: Reproductive Technologies from Artificial Insemination to Artificial Wombs* (London: Women's Press, 1988), 101–3.

27 Anon., 'Conception in a watch glass', *New England Journal of Medicine* 217 (1937), 678.

28 J. Rock, M. Menkin, '*In vitro* fertilisation and cleavage of human ovarian eggs', *Science* 100 (1944), 105–7.

29 A. T. Hertig, 'Thirty four fertilised human ova, good, bad and indifferent, recovered from 210 women of known fertility: a study of biologic wastage in early human pregnancy', *Paediatrics* 23 (1959), 202–11.

30 C. R. Austin, M. W. H. Bishop, 'Fertilisation in mammals', *Biological Reviews* 32 (1957), 296–349.

31 R. G. Edwards *et al.*, 'Early stages of fertilisation *in vitro* of human oocytes matured *in vitro*', *Nature* 221 (1969), 632–5.

32 R. G. Edwards, P. C. Steptoe, *A Matter of Life: The Story of a Medical Breakthrough* (London: Hutchinson, 1980).

33 See J. C. Fletcher, J. D. Schulman, 'Fetal research: the state of the question', *Hastings Center Report* 15 (April 1985), 6–12.

34 Department of Health and Social Security, *The Use of Fetuses and Fetal Material for Research* (Report of the Advisory Group) (London

HMSO, 667(72), 1972).

35 S. Lawler, 'Conception and development of a foetal tissue bank', *Journal of Clinical Pathology* 34 (1981), 240–8.

36 A. A. Templeton *et al.*, 'The recovery of pre-ovulatory oocytes using a fixed schedule of ovulation induction and follicle aspiration', *British Journal of Obstetrics and Gynaecology* 91 (1984), 148–54.

Chapter three

Ethics and embryology: the case for experimentation

Robert Edwards

In this chapter I wish to present briefly my own view on the ethics of work on human embryology. I write as a working scientist, who usually gets home at around 8 o'clock each evening, and has then to cope with writings on philosophy, law, and ethics of my field. I trust this will account for any lack of knowledge or expertise as a philosopher or ethicist that becomes apparent in reading this chapter.

Many of the great movements in our civilization are driven by science, and many of the most controversial ideas became evident to the scientific world long before they came to the attention of the general public. Abstract ideas turn into practical applications so that ethical problems arise in most fields of research, and enter a wide public debate. This situation has become increasingly common and widely recognized over the past few years.

In general, scientists are notoriously shy of 'ethics' in relation to the general public. Many of them do not care to enter such debates even in their own field of work unless the social circumstances literally compel them into the ethical discussion, although there have been some exceptions. Among these were the contributions of nuclear physicists to the debates on nuclear weaponry, where the initial debates were carried out between physicists with conflicting ideas about introducing such weapons. Some of the earliest arguments on genetic engineering of viruses, bacteria, plants, and animals were also stimulated by scientists, concerned about the implications of their work. Perhaps, too, in my own field, our initial contributions on its ethics, published in articles and debates in the 1960s and the 1970s, occurred long before most people knew the field even existed. Nevertheless, most scientists have never been trained in ethics, and they face considerable difficulties when faced with the formulation of their own ethical principles in relation to their subject.

The development of *in vitro* fertilization in humans and the ethical

Note: This chapter is based on a lecture delivered by Professor Edwards at the Centre for Social Ethics and Policy, University of Manchester.

implications of carrying out research on human embryos became clear some twenty years ago. By 1969, extensive research on mouse and rabbit embryos, and on human oocytes, had shown how it was possible to contemplate similar studies on human embryos, in order to carry out a number of scientific and clinical studies of potential value in medicine. One major problem remained to be solved: how to gain a simple means of access to the ovary to collect ripening human eggs. At about that time, when already committed to human embryology, I remember reading a small article by Patrick Steptoe in which he described the use of laparoscopy to approach the oviduct simply and easily, without a major operation on the patient. His approach promised to help overcome the clinical and surgical problems of *in vitro* fertilization, for it offered an easy access to ovarian follicles to collect eggs from a patient, and if necessary to replace them in the oviduct. All this happened at a most propitious time, for many embryological techniques were available from studies on mice, rabbits, and other species, and some promised a clear potential value to humans. Patrick and I agreed that it was time to go ahead with the first problem: the attempted alleviation of some forms of infertility.

At that time, there were no ethical committees for us to consult. Ethical committees were, in general, introduced later in the UK, even though they were widely used in the USA in those early years in the 1960s. The contrast between then and today is even greater, because ethics are now very much in the public eye, whereas then it was necessary to formulate our own arguments by writing articles in *Scientific American* or *Nature*, in order to stimulate debate. We did these things, but no one appeared to be greatly interested in the ethics of *in vitro* fertilization or embryo research, so we were largely left to make our own decisions about introducing and sustaining our work. At that time, I was fully aware of all the implications of cloning, hybrids between humans and animals, chimeras, and many other aspects of experimental embryology since we had studied and even introduced many of these experimental situations in animals in our own laboratories. We decided there was an urgent need to carry out studies on human embryology in order to introduce the replacement of embryos for the alleviation of infertility, and so began our collaborative study with Patrick in Oldham and me in Cambridge, which was to mean endless driving for me between Cambridge and Oldham – almost 200 miles apart! Many other studies were also possible besides the alleviation of infertility, depending on the availability of human eggs and embryos for research, including a study of the causes of chromosomal imbalance, the preimplantation diagnosis of inherited defects, relationships between cancer and embryonic cells, and many others, but we believed the most urgent was the alleviation of infertility.

We first decided it was ethically acceptable to ask infertile patients if we could collect eggs from their ovaries after mild ovarian stimulation. These patients were infertile, and current techniques were unable to help them to conceive. The intention was to introduce them into a programme of *in vitro* fertilization if and when embryo replacements became a possibility. They volunteered to accept ovarian stimulation, and to attend a hospital at a particular time in order that their eggs might be collected before ovulation. Initially, it was necessary to confirm that their oocytes were maturing in their ovaries as predicted from studies on oocytes maturing *in vitro*, and that they would ovulate at approximately thirty seven hours after the injection of human chorionic gonadotrophin (HCG). Later, it was essential to attempt to fertilize these oocytes, and grow them to blastocysts. To our delight, progress was extremely rapid in the period 1969–1970, for all our ideas on oocyte maturation, fertilization, and the growth of embryos proved to be correct, and we were able to observe oocyte maturation, the successive stages of fertilization, and the cleavage of embryos *in vitro*, all within one to two years after we began our collaboration.

Ethical problems were rising fast. We felt that some embryos growing *in vitro* had to be studied in order to ensure that their nuclear structure and their chromosomal complement was normal. This meant a delay in introducing our patients onto a programme of *in vitro* fertilization, and in attempting to alleviate their infertility by embryo replacement, but it was essential to make sure as far as we could that the embryos were growing normally *in vitro*.

Was it ethically acceptable to take eggs from our patients in this way, without any immediate promise of attempting to alleviate their infertility? Was it ethical to use their embryos for analysis, which, to my mind, were the world's first 'spare' embryos, since they were taken from patients who might hope to gain from the procedure? We felt that the clinical urgency justified the work and that there was a definite promise of treatment to the patients who volunteered their oocytes. I would like to point out that it was more than ten years before any other clinic produced human embryos of comparable quality, indicating how far ahead we were in our concepts of treating infertility during those early years.

A further ethical question arose, one which has attracted much attention since then. How long should we permit embryos to continue their growth *in vitro*? We decided that the growth of embryos to blastocysts at five days after fertilization would be a sufficient indication for embryo replacements to begin. For any further research, we felt that nine days would be acceptable, partly because this was the stage of growth where the embryo begins to implant in the uterus, so it would be unlikely to grow for much longer *in vitro*. In any case, by nine days, the embryonic disc is beginning to grow and differentiate rapidly, and we felt that enough information could be gained from these early stages of growth to convince ourselves about the normality of the embryos, and to open research into other fields of study. In the event, blastocysts were seen very soon, and we began replacing embryos in their mothers in the early 1970s.

After several years of struggle, Lesley Brown conceived and delivered her baby in 1978. The new field of human conception and human embryology was open to science and medicine. So, too, were the ethical arguments about these advances. These had really begun in the 1960s, when we began to write our own articles on the ethics of this field, and a group of critics joined in during the early 1970s, many of them hostile to *in vitro* fertilization, including Paul Ramsey, Leon Kass, James Watson, and others. They insisted that *in vitro* fertilization did not 'cure' infertility because the patients remained as infertile as ever, even after delivering a test-tube baby; or that the risk of abnormalities was so high that the work was unethical, as was research on the unborn, so that infanticide would have to be practised when babies with abnormalities developed to full term. These and other arguments did not impress us because numerous studies on animals had shown that the preimplantation embryo is highly resistant to teratogenic change, i.e. a change which tends to produce anomalies of growth, and the frequency of anomalies *in vitro* is the same as for conception *in vivo*. We felt that the urgency of treatment for patients with infertility, which has far more serious implications to health than is usually accepted, was sufficient justification to continue the work.

The birth of Louise Brown released what can only be described as an explosion of scientific and medical energy. Initially, there was a massive disbelief about test-tube babies, but as this subsided, the number of *in vitro* fertilization (IVF) centres began to increase logarithmically. Today, there are, I believe, more than 140 centres in France alone. Many clinics are successful, but others produce hardly a single baby before going into liquidation. In our own clinic, Bourn Hall, established in 1980, we have delivered more than 1000 children by now, and many more are expected. Clinics of *in vitro* fertilization have spread across the world, into India, China, Russia, Africa, and America, and there is no doubt about the urgent need of the treatment for many patients. It is a little ironic that this advance was made without our receiving any state funds for research, and also that the commitment of public monies in the U.K. e.g. from the National Health Service is severely restricted for this branch of medicine.

It is also clear now that the chances of success, i.e. of establishing a clinical pregnancy, have not improved greatly since those Oldham days. In the final series of patients there, 12.5% patients conceived following the replacement of a single embryo. In Bourn Hall today, the chance of a single embryo implanting is not much greater than 15%, and I doubt that any other clinic has a greater success. This is why two or three embryos are replaced – to raise the success of pregnancy per replacement to 33% or thereabouts. New methods have been introduced, such as GIFT, in which the eggs and sperm are placed in the oviduct, together with novel methods of intra-uterine insemination or intra-peritoneal insemination. In my view, many of these procedures might not last for much longer, because the introduction of vaginal ultrasound for the collection of oocytes has removed any need to invade the abdominal cavity to collect oocytes from patients. The embryos can also be replaced simply and quickly into the uterus without the need for anaesthesia or any major operation.

Perhaps new methods of hormone treatment might also have a major impact on the success of *in vitro* fertilization. The introduction of LHRH (Luteinizing Hormone Releasing Hormone) agonists has sharply improved success rates in several clinics. In Bourn Hall, for example, the chance of identical pregnancy with three or four embryos is sometimes as high as 40–50%, and this might be an indication that the newer methods of ovarian stimulation are more powerful than those used originally.

Some practical ethical questions have arisen which are seldom discussed. One question concerns the ages of patients, because the chances of pregnancy decline and the risk of abortion increases in patients over forty. Who should decide were the age-limit should lie, the doctor or the patient? Do patients have a right to treatment provided they are properly counselled and understand exactly the chances of success and the risks that they take in accepting treatment? This raises the old conflict between the ethics of patients and the ethics of doctors, for many doctors refuse to treat the over-forties. Another ethical issue has been largely solved, namely that raised by Paul Ramsey and others in the early 1970s. By now, it is clear that the chance of birth defects following *in vitro* fertilization is approximately the same as that following conception *in vivo*, just as we had predicted on the basis of animal studies. Nor have detailed analyses on the babies from Bourn Hall shown any consistent pattern of damage, such as would be expected if there was a specific factor leading to fetal damage.

Another ethical issue that is seldom mentioned concerns the ethics of care. Standards vary in clinics throughout the UK and throughout the world, including in the care taken in counselling, in the theatre and laboratory, with the monitoring of the patient's hormones and in whether or not patients are offered the freezing of embryos surplus to those needed for replacement. Each of these issues stimulates intense debate amongst doctors and scientists practising *in vitro* fertilization, yet they seldom appear in conference proceedings or in the press.

Most ethical concern arises, though, about research on human embryos, donating gametes, or surrogate parenthood. Parliament has already legislated on surrogacy, and may well be tempted to do so again. Concerning embryo research, it is obvious that any studies on human embryos must be restricted to those essential in clinical medicine or for clarifying fundamental aspects of human development, and the published research has conformed with this belief. I would now like to describe some of the studies in progress, before turning to a brief final comment on the ethics of the work.

Among the most urgent clinical problems is the need to discover the incidence and causes of chromosomal imbalance in human embryos. Most of these anomalies arise due to the presence of a single extra chromosome in an embryo, as in Down's syndrome, although there are many others with varying chromosomal complements. Perhaps one-quarter or one-third of all human embryos conceived *in vitro* or *utero* have one or more chromosomal imbalances and there is only limited knowledge about the causative factors. It is known that, in the case of Down's syndrome and related disorders, the defect mostly arises in the oocyte, before fertilization occurs, but it is essential to clarify why this condition arises in the first place.

The defect could arise as the oocytes are formed in the ovary, at a time when the mother is herself a fetus, or during the final stages of the growth of oocytes in the ovary in the adult mother, i.e. at ovulation or during fertilization, when chromosomal movements may go awry during these periods of rapid chromosomal transitions. Studies on the chromosomes of embryos should help to decide between these possible causes, and might help to promote methods or treatments which can help to limit or prevent such disordered growth.

A second piece of research, rapidly becoming necessary in my opinion, is to find out if embryos can be typed for specific forms of inherited disease. Cells can be dissected from animal embryos without too much difficulty (e.g. one cell from an eight-cell embryo or a piece of mural trophoblast containing ten or a dozen cells from a blastocyst) and similar techniques are being applied to the human embryo. The amount of tissue removed is very small indeed, but these excised cells could then be typed for certain genetic diseases in order to gain knowledge about the embryo they came from. Some years ago, we used this method to identify the sex of rabbit blastocysts. If similar work could be applied to the human embryo, it might help to avert the birth of children with sex-linked conditions, such as haemophilia, by replacing embryos known to be female into the mothers and so averting the birth of afflicted boys.

Further advances in this field of study await the development of DNA probes specific for particular gene defects, which are highly characterized. Some of these have already been used on intact embryos prepared for microscopy, e.g. a DNA Y-probe which has been used in order to identify the sex of intact human embryos after they were fixed and stained. Another approach, and the one that will almost certainly be the definitive method, will be to amplify the small amount of DNA in the excised cells, so that it is increased by several thousand times, to provide sufficient for routine DNA typing now extensively used in many laboratories.

For me, the ethics of such work is fundamentally utilitarian, and I would type embryos like this without hesitation if it avoided aborting an afflicted fetus at five months of gestation, which is the alternative approach to avoiding the birth of babies with inherited disorders. I accept that rejecting embryos found to be afflicted would not be therapeutic as far as the embryo is concerned, even if it is for the couple themselves. The most important ethical point is to avert the birth of a severely handicapped baby, and this to my mind far outweighs the ethical disadvantage of discarding a cleaving embryo or a blastocyst. For this reason, I find it difficult to accept the legislation in Victoria, Australia, which bans all research on embryos unless it is therapeutic for the embryo itself. Their decision could compel couples to continue aborting fetus at five months of gestation instead of attempting to identify abnormalities at five days post-fertilization. Likewise, opposition to embryo typing in France has been based on objections to the premeditated selection of certain types of embryos which are replaced in their mothers and given a chance of life, whereas the others are destroyed. In this case, the critics argue that this is the first step towards 'choosing' those human embryos which will live or die, and the implication is, I suppose, that choice will ultimately extend to other characteristics, perhaps even including physical or mental characteristics. Their objection seems to be a 'slippery slope' type of argument, where the advantages of eliminating disease are discarded through fears of an uncertain eugenic future.

Freezing eggs and embryos also raises problems in ethics. There are doubts about the wisdom of storing embryos for ten years or more or about donating them to recipients if they are no longer needed by their parents. Yet freezing is simply an essential adjunct to *in vitro* fertilization, for ten or twenty embryos can be frozen for a patient, then replaced in ten or twenty successive menstrual cycles, raising the chance of pregnancy. Once again, the utilitarian argument appeals to me. Some scientists even suggest collecting as many eggs as possible and freezing them all, so the patient returns through successive menstrual cycles for all her embryos, one by one, until she becomes pregnant. No doubt this approach will work one day, and it might be simple and effective.

One of the most complex dilemmas about research concerns the origin of the embryos used for study. This has led to argument about the ethics of 'spare' embryos and 'research' embryos, a debate that split The Warnock Committee. There is an important distinction for us between spare embryos and research embryos. Spare embryos include those that have been fertilized by two spermatozoa, or have too many pronuclei at fertilization, or have other anomalies during cleavage. Another source of spare embryos arises from patients who no longer require their frozen-stored embryos and donate them for research. All of these eggs have been fertilized *in vitro*, and the intention was to obtain embryos for replacement, but in each case such a replacement has become impossible. In other words, the mother would not wish them replaced, because they might lead to an abnormal child, or because she has become too old or changed her mind about accepting her frozen embryos. In a sense, she has 'aborted' these embryos, which opens an argument that the rules about the use of tissues from aborted fetuses should also apply to these embryos. I must emphasize here that all the embryos growing normally *in vitro* from every patient, and not needed for replacement as fresh embryos, are frozen-stored in case the parents should want them to establish a pregnancy at a later date.

Research embryos are different. They are conceived purely for research by asking patients to donate an egg, which is fertilized by a spermatozoon from any man, and the resulting embryo is simply designed to be fitted into an experimental protocol. With the current method of hormone stimulation, it is possible to obtain twenty or thirty eggs from a woman, and so produce a large number of embryos. I am aware of the argument that research on a spare or abnormal embryo is morally equivalent to research on any other 'research' embryo but I find it difficult to accept research embryos for a different reason. This objection applies to the intent of scientists specifically to create such embryos purely for research, even before the egg donor is given her hormones for ovarian stimulation. Making decisions about producing embryos especially for research is a step for Parliament, not the individual scientist working in a laboatory to further his research. My argument is somewhat analogous to the rules of utilizing tissue from human abortuses, where the scientists requiring the tissue has no involvement whatsoever in the patient's decision to have an abortion. It is interesting to note that the Voluntary Licensing Authority in Britain accepts research embryos, whereas virtually every other ethical committee in Europe, Australia, and the United States refuses to permit this practice. So here we have a conflict between ethical committees!

Let me briefly discuss another aspect of embryo research which raises complex ethical debates, namely the limit to their growth *in vitro*. I will not deal with the technicalities of this work, but merely with some of the concepts that emerge from it. A considerable amount of information could be gained from studies on embryos after day five. Embryonic cells have some properties that are similar to cancer cells. Studies on embryonic tissues might reveal some of the underlying systems regulating cell differentiation, and the nature of organogenesis of an individual from the embryo's genetic blueprint. Some forms of human development are anomalous, and cause disastrous malformations early in growth: the onset of these disorders in one cell or a group of cells can now be traced by modern techniques of molecular biology, so that the lineage of such anomalous cell lines can be identified, even perhaps to one or a few stem cells in the embryo. All of this work will clarify our under-standing of ourselves, and of disorders in growth; none of it is designed to introduce cloning or deliberately to modify the inherited characteristics of man.

Another example, provided by our own work in mice, concerns the use of embryonic cells for grafting into sick adults. In mice, cells can be taken from outgrowths of blastocysts, or from fetuses implanted on day 6 of pregnancy, and used to repair the effects of lethal irradiation in adult mice, or to modify the expression of certain disordered genes affecting the blood system. It is even possible to use cells from a rat embryo to repair these mice, for there is no problem with rejection when donor cells are taken from such early-developing embryos. It is also possible that cells from human abortuses will colonize mice, for initial results indicate that this system will work too. In other words, here is a simple means of grafting without the need to obtain bone marrow from volunteers, which offers a safe rapid and successful colonization using the earliest-forming cells of the blood system. The advantages could be immense, especially in these days when new genetic characteristics could be inserted into these cells to make them even more efficient. It is even possible that other organs may be cured, such as ovary, liver or pancreas, and it is worth noting that neural tissues are forming rapidly during these early stages of growth. The possibility of transplanting fetal brain cells into patients with Huntington's chorea or Alzheimer's disease is a variant on this approach, using tissues which are already highly differentiated from abortuses much later in gestation.

Should such studies be encouraged? They have become highly topical, since the public has become suddenly aware of the use of tissues from animals to repair man – a field that has been in existence for many years – and of the value of transplanting brain tissues to patients with severe neurological disorders. The embryos would have to grow to stages where these cells differentiate, and many cells would be needed for transplantation. In effect, this means the use of tissue from embryos aged from 20–25 days, although it may one day be possible to use cells from earlier stages. The Warnock Committee suggested that research on embryos was permissible only up to day fourteen, arguing that the appearance of the primitive streak was a fundamental step in embryonic growth. In my opinion, rules like that cannot be made about embryology, which is a gradual process of steady change, for there are no specific days here or there which can be used to justify a belief that something new and fundamental has occurred, and which indicates without any doubt that research should then end. Perhaps the need to grow embryos beyond day fifteen is less urgent now, for a new abortifacient called RU 486 expels intact fetuses at all stages of gestation, and tissue can now be obtained from abortuses in these early stages of growth. Another reason why research after day fourteen may not be so vital is that undifferentiated animal cells can be grown *in vitro* for years on end, yet they are capable of differentiating into all the adult tissues of the body under the right conditions, e.g. when placed in a growing embryo.

There are obviously major ethical arguments raised about the limit to research on human embryos. Absolutists, such as those in the Roman Catholic Church, will never accept any research after the moment of 'fertilization', whatever that means. There can be no doubt that we will be fortunate if Parliament accepts day fourteen as an arbitrary limit to research. Some commentators, many of them philosophers, argue that embryonic growth proceeds from a 'biological' stage to 'personhood', and they object to research only when the embryo becomes a person in their eyes. Unfortunately, this transition is so late in gestation, or even after birth, that such arguments do not help with the ethics of *in vitro* fertilization.

In this chapter I have obviously taken a consequentialist viewpoint to justify research on embryos. Perhaps it is not too difficult to be a utilitarian in this field of research, when fetuses of a much later age are aborted in hundreds of thousands with the blessings of State and Church, which obviously qualifies objections to embryo research from these quarters. Nevertheless, we must expect objections to or arguments against many of the concepts outlined in this chapter for they raise questions about the value and rights of human life, and a society would be judged to be deficient in moral debate if it did not express its doubts. Do we have a duty to do all we can to save or improve the life of a severely afflicted child or adult, who already exists as a living person and could possibly be helped by the use of differentiating tissues from embryos? Can we establish research embryos in our laboratories without expecting public criticism? Is society becoming too tolerant, 'conditioned' by the obvious advantages of research as infertility becomes less of a scourge, as organ and cell grafting becomes ever more widespread? Will society even change so far as to question the birth of children with severe inherited disease and raise doubts about the responsibility of parents who fail to avoid such a situation?

Even though I am being obviously pragmatic, I would not wish to give the impression that scientists do not exert their own very tight rules and standards about their work. Some of our rules should perhaps be classified and stated more firmly than they are. We believe it is unjustified to do work with human embryos if the necessary information can come from animals. I believe that any specific research on an embryo should be restricted to the earliest stage of growth, when it can be accomplished, and this is where a day fourteen rule could be a possible disadvantage. If legal permission is given to day fourteen, then scientists might be tempted to grow embryos to that day in order to gain the maximum possible information about embryonic growth, even though answers to their questions could be gained by day five or day six. I believe that a third rule is needed: there must be a separate justification for each piece of research; it must have a clear objective, reasons must be presented why it is important, and why it cannot be achieved using animals, and descriptions should be given of the methods that will have to be employed.

The movement of science into today's society has transformed it beyond belief, opening opportunities for industrial, veterinary, and clinical research, but also establishing a set of moral values which would not have emerged otherwise. Many of its concepts challenge existing values or standards of treatment, and so inevitably conflict with older standards, so that a choice must be made between the old and the new. Science inevitably challenges so many beliefs, including religious beliefs, for the concepts of Darwinism, the evolution of the universe, the periodic table of the elements, and the laws of thermodynamics form a basis to a set of values which are, for me, far more fundamental than those established by the concepts of the Virgin Birth or the Resurrection. And conflicts will also inevitably arise as science moves into medicine, bringing ideas which antagonize established ideas on life. This is shown by the reported comments of the Archbishop of Melbourne in 1982, who could not accept *in vitro* fertilization and its consequences: 'God has bound the transmission of life to the conjugal sex act ... if science seeks to exclude or substitute the marital act the scientific action is not licit.'

Can he be right? And can conception be limited to intercourse? The overwhelming consensus of society today would not support his viewpoint. And how can we judge the value of early embryonic life itself? Is fertilization essential as a marker of 'human-ness'? As a scientist, I am aware that life may be initiated without a spermatozoon, through parthenogenesis, or formed abnormally such as in the case of the hydatidiform mole which arises from the nucleus of a single spermatozoon without any chromosomal complement from the egg. Again speaking as a scientist, it seems unwise and even not permissible to restrict society's ethical protection of an embryo from the moment of fertilization, and to remove such protection from the gametes, for this could have disastrous consequences. Many geneticists and embryologists would argue that it is genetically acceptable to 'tailor' the somatic cells of the body – the kidney, heart, brain, and other tissue, because such tailoring will perish at death. On the other hand, genetic modifications to the germ cells could release new genes into the human gene pool, and this could have consequences beyond the imagination of the researchers. It might even be more important to protect the gametes than perhaps any other organ, a viewpoint in total conflict with that of the Roman Catholic Church.

In case it seems that I am specifically criticizing theologians and organized religion, let me add two further points. I believe that any scientist who understands his work must be fundamentally religious, although not necessarily in the sense of classical religion. Science uncovers the work and art of a grand designer, exposing a reality of such sheer beauty and economy that it drives many scientists to become totally immersed in their work. Secondly, it is clear that many theologians query the basis of their own philosophical and theological beliefs, and that many of them – including Roman Catholics – accept that new theological truths will be discovered through science and technology. Among these (and a lack of space demands that this list must necessarily be highly limited) are Lord Soper who declared in the House of Lords that the truths of science help him to a greater depth of theological understanding, Charles

Curran in the United States, a broadminded Catholic theologian who was banned by the Vatican from teaching, the Bishop of Durham, and others like them. Many other theologians too are prepared to accept embryo research and even surrogate mothers, when they have understood the implications of such work.

Where and when will all these debates end? Perhaps in a parliamentary decision to restrict embryo research to virtually nothing, as proposed in Mr Enoch Powell's Unborn Children's Protection Bill of a few years ago, or to prevent surrogacy completely. Mr Powell's Bill tried to insist on the need for infertile couples to gain the Secretary of State's permission to undergo *in vitro* fertilization, and this attempt to impose a political decision on couples seeking to have a child must surely be one of the most serious infringements of individual rights ever to be placed before the Mother of Parliaments.

Virtually all the countries of the Western world have considered or passed legislation on *in vitro* fertilization and its consequences, or have delegated authority to a national ethical committee for decisions to be made on an *ad hoc* basis. Since the field is moving so rapidly, I believe that national ethical committees offer by far the best solution, because they would help to avoid passing legislation too soon, which would have to be changed or repealed in such a highly fluid situation of new research findings and fresh clinical opportunities.

As I glance over what I have written, I see so many fascinating aspects of the ethics of *in vitro* fertilization and embryo research that have not been considered or even mentioned for lack of space. These include the role of scientists and others in decision making, or a deeper consideration of the relationships between the ethics of doctors and of their patients. I have barely mentioned surrogacy, and some aspects of the work such as embryo donation and child donation have not even been raised at all. Neither has the need or otherwise for a mother to give her permission to use the tissues of her aborted fetus or her spare embryos – such consent almost constitutes virtually a double wrong since she has already condemned the fetus or embryo to death – nor the vexed questions of known versus unknown donors of gametes, or the debate about the number of embryos to be replaced. And, as I feared at the beginning of this chapter, I have not been able to do justice to the respective viewpoints of many commentators on the fundamentals of their philosophy, such as the balance between reason and feelings, the role of law or the power of pressure groups, of women's liberation and of professional organizations. Perhaps enough has been written, though, to stimulate the debate, and these overlooked topics must await a future debate.

Chapter four

The case against experimentation

John Marshall

Despite the title of this essay I ought to say, at the outset, that I am in no way opposed to research. As well as being a medical doctor, I am a scientist. I therefore recognize that research is a very important way by which we advance our knowledge and which in turn enables us to help people with their illnesses and their problems of many kinds. Research, which is an organized way of proceeding with the advance of knowledge, is very necessary. But I must immediately enter a caveat, namely that research is something which cannot be allowed to be pursued simply for its own sake. It must be constrained by the same sort of ethical principles by which we constrain our other activities in life. This may seem a rather obvious statement to have to make, but one finds that some people seem to think that the mere fact that some activity is for research justifies the activity in itself.

What then do I mean by research in this context? It is very important to be clear what is meant, because in one sense any medical intervention is research. Giving an aspirin to a patient, though done thousands and thousands of times, may on the thousand-and-oneth occasion produce some unexpected, unpredictable result because of idiosyncrasies in that patient. Therefore, when people talk on the one hand about certain orthodox procedures which they do without thinking and, on the other hand, about unorthodox procedures, it is clear that there is a difference in degree but never a difference in kind. Anything that is done, any intervention in another person, can have unexpected and unpredictable results. But it is not about that that we are really talking in this context.

The other area which ought to be distinguished is that of improving therapy. Again, people think that there is a certain standard way of doing appendicectomies, or coronary by-pass procedures, that there is a certain standard way of treating people with respiratory failure. But medicine is always engaged in the business of improving therapy, and improving therapy is often on a research basis. When you try to modify some procedure because you think it might work better in a different way, you are engaged in a form of research, a form of enquiry. This again is not the question which I am addressing here, though again it has its own ethical boundaries.

In the particular context of embryo experimentation, which is the subject of this volume, I am concerned with that type of research which of its nature leads to the destruction of the embryo. This occurs because people are seeking to gain further knowledge of the embryo by examining its chromosomes, or its biochemical content, or some other aspect. This is the area which I am about to consider. I am *not* discussing improvements of therapy which do not lead to the destruction of the embryo. I am referring to that area of study and research in which, as part of the research, you must inevitably destroy the entity in order to gain the knowledge that you want.

Now of course research has very many facets which there is not space to discuss here. But they can often be reduced to two major issues. First of all, *what is done*, and second, *why it is being done*. It is with regard to the first issue that we reach the nub of the question about experimentation on embryos. It may appear perfectly easy to determine what is done. Let us look at an example. One person says he has a clump of cells which he is squashing between two slides in order to count the chromosomes or to see whether they have got short arms or other aberrations. That is all he is doing – looking at a clump of cells which he is squashing in order to count chromosomes. Another person doing or watching exactly the same physical procedure says, 'No, that is not what you are doing, what you are doing is killing a human being'. So it is immediately clear that the question of *what is being done* is much more complex than appears at first sight. It is not enough simply to stand by the laboratory bench and observe the physical manoeuvres that are being carried out. It is necessary to take a step beyond that. This brings me to the heart of the question which I want to address in this chapter.

In this sphere it can be quite useful to move away from the scientist and look to the man in the street because he, interested in this very important issue, asks the question, 'When does human life begin?'. He says, 'If you can tell me when human life begins, then I will vote for no experimentation after that point and for experimentation before that point'. It appears a very simple, straightforward approach. But when this question 'when does human life begin?' is addressed, it becomes clear that it needs further refining and nuancing. After all, the sperm is alive and comes from the human species. The ovum is alive and comes from the human species. When sperm and ovum come together in the conceptus, that is clearly alive and belongs to the human species. So in all these human life extends way back to the sperm, the ovum, and certainly to the conceptus. But that is not really the question that the man in the street is asking when he says, 'When does human life begin?', or 'Tell me when human life begins, and then I can make my decisions about it'. The question he is *really* asking is, 'When did I, John Marshall, come into being?', 'When did I as a person come into existence?', which is a different question from 'When did a certain stage in this biological development happen?'.

Now the former question, as will be recognized, is not a scientific question. It is no use looking to the scientist to answer it. It is no use hoping that bigger and better electron microscopes will ultimately be able to see when John Marshall started. It is essentially a philosophical question and, for those of a theistic disposition, a philosophical question which will have theological overtones. It is very important to recognize this because the scientists are trying to determine the question purely in scientific terms, while many of the non-scientists are hoping that the scientists will provide them with this basic datum on which they can act. But this is not how it is going to be. The question of when I, John Marshall, came into existence is one which is quite outside the capability of science to answer. Of course people try to answer it in a variety of different ways. Some say that it is at the time of fertilization or at the moment of implantation or at the moment of quickening. Perhaps some say it is even as late as birth. But people will answer this question in a different way during the biological development of this entity which ultimately everybody will accept as being John Marshall, or at least as the anatomical substrate of John Marshall. So there is no way in which one person can say that his or her own particular *way* of answering the question is right.

I have said that the scientist cannot answer the question for us. But this is not to say that we can go about answering the question quite irrespective of the scientific data. We have to look at the scientific data and reflect upon it before making our philosophical or theological determination. Thus, scientific information is an important input into, even though it does not ultimately answer, the question. It is, therefore, important that I rehearse very briefly the essential scientific facts on which we can then reflect.

The sperm and the ovum come together, fertilization takes place, and then multiplication begins to two cells, four cells, eight cells, sixteen cells, and so on. At a certain stage in this clump of cells, clefts or spaces appear so that you end up with, as it were, something rather like a figure 8. (This is a very simplified version of the process, but it will do perfectly well; it is accurate in the basic biological facts and it will serve well for our present purposes.) The cells on the upper part of the 8 are going to burrow into the wall of the uterus and enable implantation to take place; the lower part of the 8 is going to provide nutrition. Where the two loops of the 8 meet, you have the so-called embryonic plate on which is situated the primitive streak from which the body will ultimately develop. This clump of cells is going to develop into tissues such as the placenta, which can quite happily be discarded after the child is born without giving it a thought. But other parts will develop into the body, the substrate, of this person who eventually will achieve maturity.

Now those who take the view that the human person comes into existence during fertilization, when looking at the clump of cells, say, 'Ah well, we accept that some of these cells are going to become placenta and so on, but somewhere in that clump of cells you are going to find one cell or two cells that ultimately will become the substrate of John Marshall'. This is not so. What happens to this clump of cells is that those on the outside will be the ones that burrow and make a placenta and those on the inside become ultimately the body of the person. But in a mouse certainly – and it is likely to be the same in humans – if you get this clump of cells before implantation has taken place and, as it were, turn it inside out, then the cells that were outside and would have become the placenta now become the body, whereas the cells that were on the inside and would have become the body now become the placenta. In other words, at this early stage all these cells are totipotential. They all have the capability of becoming anything related to this developing entity. It is their position in the mass, as far as can be seen, and their topographical relationship to neighbouring structures, which determine whether they become tissues which can be thrown away without any compunction when they have served their purpose, or whether they become the basis of the person. So it would not be true to say that somewhere right at the beginning there are one or two cells which ultimately will form the anatomical substrate of the person. At this stage any of those cells are capable of doing that.

Another phenomenon which goes along the same lines is revealed when one of these cells is detached – say at the eight- or sixteen-cell stage – and successfully cultured. This cell will then become a separate person. So potentially you will have a separate person, but also of course an identical person, and therefore an identical twin. This totipotentiality is of great importance at this early stage. But as the process goes on, differentiation takes place. The primitive streak appears which is going to be the substrate of the body and, as time goes on, different cells of the primitive streak will become different organs, the brain, the heart, the kidneys. It is a progressive process of differentiation.

So the biological facts are that the sperm alone or the ovum alone will never become the basis of a person. Once they have come together and start to multiply, then the cells initially have toti-potential, that is they can become part of the person, part of the membranes or, if we separate them off, become a separate person. As time goes by, increasing differentiation takes place so that ultimately cells are set in one line and cannot become anything else. These are the biological facts on which we have to reflect. Those who maintain that the person is there from the moment of fertilization or from the period of fertilization will, on this basis, obviously reject experimentation that leads to destruction, because for them it is exactly equivalent to destroying something we recognize as a person walking along the street. Whereas someone who takes the other view will point to this non-differentiated state of the entity and the progressive differentiation that ensues. He will arbitrarily say – and I don't mean 'arbitrarily' in the pejorative sense – 'I am going to accord to this entity those rights, take those duties upon myself which I owe to it, which I would give to a person'. Some would say this when the primitive streak appears; some would say this when implantation occurs; some would say it later. It is on this that a judgement has to be made, a personal judgement as to what stand one is going to take, because there is certainly no *scientific* answer. Moreover, for those who are of a theistic persuasion, there is no *revealed* answer to this. The great religions of the world certainly have a very firm position about it, but it is a position which they have attained through rationalization, not through revelation. They cannot fall back on saying 'this has been revealed and, as far as we are concerned, this is what we believe'. It is therefore something on which everybody has to reflect and then to reach their own appropriate conclusion.

What steps have to be taken to articulate the case against experimentation? In The Warnock Committee which the Government set up to address the whole business of embryo research there was, as you probably know, a majority and a minority about embryo experimentation, and I was one of the minority opposing experimentation. This was not because I felt that I could decide that a person was there from the moment of fertilization. I do not think that is a question one can firmly answer. Moreover, if one looks at the Christian tradition, one can see that the present very firm position held by some of the Christian churches is not the position they have always held. They thought, in past times, that there was an evolution in the development of each individual through what were called the vegetative, animal and finally human stage. The idea of ensoulment, or the embryo becoming human in the full sense happening at a later stage in development, was very widely and respectably held, not just by theologians. But it is also true to say that although belief in delayed animation, delayed ensoulment, was widely held, this did not deny that respect and care must be given to the entity before that point.

The minority view on Warnock was that experimentation should not be allowed, not because we felt we could decide that the person came into being at the moment of fertilization, but because this entity clearly has the potential to become a person – potential which we felt it wrong to destroy. This is a very important distinction. People might think it is splitting hairs to make the distinction between saying it *is* a person and saying that it has the *potential to become a person*. The reason the minority took this view was because we felt, as I have tried to explain, that the decision as to when the entity becomes a person is one which will never in fact be resolved. It is a matter really of personal decision after reflecting philosophically and theologically upon the biological facts. The matter could not, however, be left in a limbo. If a decision has to be made in this uncertainty as to when the event or process of becoming a person took place or started, it is necessary to adopt an attitude to the entity before that time. And since it has quite clearly the potential to become a person, we therefore felt that experimentation or research, in the sense that I defined it at the beginning, should not be allowed.

Now this point of view has been challenged on several grounds, understandably, as every aspect of this subject has been challenged. One of the challenges concerns the word 'potential'. People say that the protein molecules which make up the *sperm* have the potential to become a person: why are you making such an issue of the potential from the particular point of fertilization? In response to that question, I accept that the sperm has the potential to become a person, but there is a difference not just in degree but in kind of qualitative difference here. The sperm can be kept for a thousand years in whatever media you wish and it will never become the anatomical substrate of a person. But if the conceptus is kept in the appropriate environment, then it will ultimately become a person. So I judge that there is a marked difference between the nature of the potential enjoyed by either the sperm alone, or the ovum alone, and that of the conceptus, the fertilized ovum. This is a very clear distinction. I conclude that those who try to blur that distinction, who say that all these entities have got potential ultimately to become this person, are making a mistake.

The other argument that is advanced against the notion of 'potentiality' is that the fertilized ovum in the dish will not become a person if it is just left there. It will develop to a certain stage and then die. In the present state of knowledge, it has to be implanted in the womb if it is going to have this chance. Therefore they say that it is nonsense to talk about potential in the way that I have done. I do not judge this to be at all a valid argument, because a distinction has to be drawn between what capability the entity has within itself, and what it receives from the environment. We can imagine that all the people who read this page regard one another as persons. Now if somebody were to exhaust all the oxygen from the rooms in which they sit, the people is those rooms would all most certainly perish. Does this mean to say that we are not persons because we cannot survive without the environment? So, to say that the fertilized ovum is not, or cannot be, a person or a potential person because, if you leave it in the dish, it is not going to survive, seems to me not at all a valid argument.

Why should the potential to become a person be regarded as so important that one would oppose experimentation on the embryo, even though the experimentation might bring valuable knowledge? I shall answer this in two parts – first, why should it be that *this* potential is so important? I believe that all life is important and by that I mean human life, animal life, plant life, and so on, although I am not one of those extremists who would not kill a fly or would weep if I saw a tree felled to the ground. But I do think that life is one of the most amazing and dramatic things. I am sure that anyone who saw the landing of the first man on the moon and, having recovered from the amazement of seeing him standing there with his machine, than watched the camera pan over that interminable waste with not a tree or a flower or a blade of grass, must have been forcibly reminded of how important, how valuable, life is. Moreover, I take the view that we have been profligate in our attitude to, and use of, life. But I suspect that this is probably beginning to change. The whole business of conservation has as its central motivating force this amazement at, and reverence for, life. In animal experimentation, whereas in the past people took no account of how many mice or rats they used for their experiments, now they are more conscious, not simply because of the cost, but because they are more aware of the importance of the conservation of life.

Thus, I judge this to be an important issue. There is a peculiar paradox in our society at the present time with regard to how people rate life. On the one hand, they destroy thousands of fetuses/embryos per year by abortion, in the majority of instances for reasons which at best are matters of convenience rather than of health. Yet, on the other hand, high-tech medicine will fight and struggle for hours, days and weeks, in a way which is quite marvellously impressive, to help a prematurely-born baby to survive. So I detect at present an ambivalence in our society in our attitude to life. On the one hand, people go to extraordinary lengths to try to preserve life – sometimes life which is almost spent – using high-tech procedures. (I sometimes ask myself, perhaps unfairly, whether people are more concerned about the development of their high technology than they are about the life.) Yet, on the other hand, we are profligate in our destruction of life. Because of this, it seems certain to me that allowing experimentation on entities which have the potential to become human beings is not the way forward.

Now in saying this, I and my colleagues who signed the minority report recognized that we were going to block some areas of advance of knowledge. And this is the second part of my answer. We did not take the head-in-the-sand attitude and say all this knowledge can be gained by other means. We fully recognized that there was going to be a loss. But we felt that the loss was not disproportionate to the gain. Since then, some scientists have joined the public relations bandwagon in overstating to the public what can be gained by embryo experimentation. Broad sweeping statements are made about the 'relief of infertility' – some parts of which I would accept – and particularly about the relief of genetic disease and handicap. This is conveyed in a way which again leaves the man in the street with the idea that, given a little embryo research, all sorts of conditions such as cystic fibrosis and other diseases are going to vanish from our society. This is not the case at all. In most of the genetically-expressed diseases, there is an abnormal gene. But, then, the gene has its mode of expression, and the intervention to correct these things is most likely to come at the point of the gene expression, when it begins to express, say, a faulty protein, switching on when it should be switching off and vice versa. The abnormality of cystic fibrosis cannot be studied until the epithelium has developed so that then the abnormalities in the secretion of mucus can be studied. We should note that this comes at a much later stage down the line, long after the fourteen days indicated by Warnock, up to which experimentation was going to be allowed.

So it seems that the scientists have rather abandoned their strictly scientific attitude and joined the public relations exercise. This is understandable because I think that nobody was more surprised than they when they saw the reception accorded to the Warnock Report. Certainly no-one was more surprised than I, because I had felt that in signing the minority report I was going to be a voice in the wilderness, but that I had made my point and that was it. I expected that the bandwagon would certainly move forward towards this brave new world of new scientific endeavour. I suspect that everybody was rather taken aback at the public response and attitude, at the widespread anxiety as to whether this *should* be the way forward or not. This was reflected in the first bill in the House of Commons when there were three-hundred-and-some members present on a Friday afternoon – a thing unheard of in the House of Commons, when everybody is usually back in their constituency. It showed the wide degree of interest and led to a two-to-one majority in favour of banning experimentation. So I surmise that the advocates of experiments were rather taken aback by this and began to think that they would have to push their case harder and further. In doing so, I judge that sometimes they made statements which were not strictly untrue, but which certainly required nuancing. I cite, for instance, the opinion poll in which the second question, quoted in the CIBA Symposium,[1] was 'Would you allow experimentation on embryos which would lead to the relief of handicap?'. Obviously the vast majority of the population is likely to say yes when it is presented in that way. The fact that experimentation is very unlikely to lead to relief of handicap was not part of the question. Thus, people were presented with artificial choices to a certain extent.

The other way in which the scientists have clearly shown that they are under some pressure and that they are fighting back is seen in the introduction of the term 'pre-embryo'. The term 'pre-embryo' was not heard of prior to all this debate. From the time of fertilization up to about the eighth week the entity was called 'embryo'. Suddenly this term 'pre-embryo' is now in every paper and every symposium. Some scientists are saying that they had been thinking along these lines already in 1975. It is surprising that if they had been thinking about it as far back as 1975, they never actually used the term until now. It seems like a public relations manoeuvre to make people think that the experts are against *embryo* experimentation, but that it is alright to experiment on the 'pre-embryo', as if the latter was somehow different.

Why then do I oppose experimentation of the kind that I have defined, namely experiments which lead to the destruction of the entity? It is because I regard the potential to become a human person as of tremendous importance, particularly in our society where there is a certain ambivalence about, and paradoxical attitude towards, life. In opposing experimentation I recognize and do not hide the fact that some advances in knowledge will be lost, but I do assert that those advances are not so great as the scientists would have us believe. I do not therefore hold that the gain is commensurate with the loss. This really is the basis of the argument.

In summary, I argue that each person has to decide in their own mind at what point in the development of this entity one is going to accord to it the status of a person. It is no use looking to the scientist or the philosopher or anybody else to give the answer. It is a judgement which individuals have to make because it is a philosophical-cum-theological judgement about which there has not been revelation, and to which one just has to apply one's mind and thought, using the broad principles with which one guides one's ethical conduct. If one comes to the decision that a person comes into being at a certain stage, then clearly this will affect one's attitude towards experimentation. On the other hand, one can conclude that this is a question which cannot be decided universally, and that each person will have their own view. On this argument, because the entity has the potential to become a person, one affirms that it should *not* be interfered with, that *nothing* should be done that prevents it realizing that potential, and things *can* be done which will help it to attain that potential. Therefore one opposes experimentation. At this point I rest my case.

Note

1   The Ciba Foundation (1986) *Human Embryo Research, Yes or No?*, London and Yew York: Tavistock Publications.

Chapter five

Embryos and hedgehogs: on the moral status of the embryo

John Harris

The question of whether or not we should permit research on or using the human embryo and indeed whether it is permissible to use the embryo or embryonic tissue for experimental or therapeutic purposes is about as vexed a question as one could hope to find. There are a number of perspectives from which one might approach such questions. There is for example a distinctive feminist approach which 'does not recognize the embryo as a separate human entity. It makes women and the social context central to its position.'[1] Equality there is what might be called the strictly utilitarian approach which sees the issue simply in cost-benefit terms and wants to trade off the moral costs in terms of people's sensibilities about the treatment of embryos with the benefits to humanity that research will bring. Then there are those who see the issue simply in terms of the rights of the embryos and regard the question as settled by the 'fact' that the embryo is a human being and so possesses 'human rights'.

Whatever the perspective from which one approaches these questions, there is one unavoidable and central issue and that is what we might call the moral status of the embryo. For what one might be entitled to do with or to an embryo will depend on its moral importance or status in precisely the same way as it does for the rest of us. The protections that surround you and me, in virtue of which we cannot simply be used or experimented upon without our consent, derive from the moral differences there are between us and other creatures. So that if the embryo is of a moral importance comparable with that of, say, normal adult human beings then the moral rights and protections possessed by such beings extend to the embryo. If it would be wrong to experiment on normal adults without their consent or to use them simply as tissue and organ banks, then it would be wrong to treat embryos likewise. Therefore when feminists say they do not recognize the embryo as a separate human entity, this is respectable only if it is the conclusion of a moral argument which addresses the question of what status the human embryo should have.

This then is the first question that must be answered. But if we can answer it there may still be further considerations that properly bear on the permissibility of experiments on embryos and these we shall consider later. First then, can we determine the moral status of the embryo?

Embryos and persons

Mary Warnock is a philosopher who has been enormously influential on the question of what it is permissible to do to and with embryos, both of course in her role as Chairman of The Warnock Committee[2] and in her many subsequent writings about embryos. In a recent major essay entitled *Do Human Cells Have Rights?*[3] Mary Warnock addresses the central question before us now. She starts with the issue of whether or not the question of the moral status of the embryo is the same question as whether or not the embryo is a person. She notes that there is a natural presumption that 'if it can be shown that the embryo *is* a person, then it will follow that it has rights, for certainly all persons have rights, and, it is sometimes held, only persons have them'.[4] She thinks this approach mistaken for reasons it is as well to be clear about at the outset of the discussion.

Taking as her point of departure an earlier discussion of mine[5] on this point, Warnock comments:

> John Harris of Manchester University ... argued that to ask whether using human embryos should be permitted or not, and for how long, is to ask *when human life begins to have moral significance*. With this I would completely agree. But he goes on to say that this question is the *same* as the question when does an embryo become a person? And here I think that confusion is likely to set in. For the question about *moral significance*, the question that is, *when do embryos morally matter*, is quite obviously one that must be answered by judgement and decision, according to a particular moral standpoint. It is not a question of fact but a question of value. How much *should* we value human life in its very early stages? But to translate this into a question about whether or not in its early stages an embryo *is a person* looks like translating this into a question of fact ... That personhood, its possession or non possession, is as much a question of value as is the question when human life begins to matter, is hard for people to grasp.

With small cavils that are irrelevant to our present discussion I agree with what Warnock says here and indeed I was using 'person' in just this sense as a shorthand term for all the reasons we have for thinking particular individuals morally important. For me and for Warnock the question of whether or not an individual is a person is the question of whether it is morally important and in particular of whether it shares whatever moral importance normal adult human beings have. I doubt anyone will be confused by this, but for our present purposes we do not need the term person and I am content to re-pose Warnock's reformulation of my original question: when do embryos begin to matter morally?

Moral significance

The question then is, when if at all, and in virtue of what, does the human embryo begin to matter morally? There are only two sorts of answer that might be given to this question. One is in terms of what the embryo *is*, that is, in terms of some description of its morally relevant features. The other is in terms of what it will *become*, that is, in terms of its *potential* for acquiring morally relevant features. These two approaches seem to have a natural tendency to collapse one into the other as we shall see, but I shall start by trying to keep them distinct.

What is the embryo?

From this perspective the moral importance of the embryo might derive from different sorts of things that might be said about it. One strategy is to attempt to give an account of the sorts of features or capacities that might make for moral relevance and see which of them apply to the embryo at particular stages of its development. The other is to locate moral importance in one resounding central principle. In a famous essay on Leo Tolstoy, called *The Hedgehog and the Fox*, Isaiah Berlin[6] takes a fragment of Greek poetry and uses it to create a celebrated typology of human thought. 'The fox knows many things, but the hedgehog knows one big thing.' There are those, according to Berlin, who pursue many ideas and those who like to bring everything under one central vision or organizing principle. The latter are hedgehogs, the former are foxes.

The embryo is a hedgehog

The slogan 'human life begins at conception' nicely captures the hedgehog's approach to the moral status of the embryo. The hedgehog believes that what matters morally is being a member of the human species and that membership begins at conception.

Now of course in one sense this is simply false. The human egg is alive well before conception and indeed it undergoes a process of development without which conception would be impossible. The sperm too is alive. In one sense then life is properly seen not as beginning but as a continuous process that proceeds uninterrupted from generation to generation.

Well, if not human life, then at least the new human individual begins at conception. Again, this is at best a misleading claim. A number of things may begin at conception. Fertilization can result in the development not of an embryo but of a tumour, called a hydatidiform mole, which can threaten the mother's life.

Even when fertilization is on the right lines it does not result in an individual. The fertilized egg becomes a cell mass which eventually divides into two major components: the embryoblast and the trophoblast. 'The embryoblast becomes the fetus and the trophoblast becomes the extraembryonic membranes, the placenta and the umbilical cord. The trophoblastic derivatives are alive, are human, and have the same genetic composition as the fetus and are discarded at birth.'[7]

A further complication is that the fertilized egg cannot be considered a new individual because it may well become two individuals; this splitting to become 'twins' can happen as late as two weeks after conception.

The idea of human life having a beginning is clearly problematic. It is more plausible to regard it as a continuum with the individual human emerging gradually. If what matters morally is human life, we are faced with the problem of protecting all human life including unfertilized human eggs and sperm. On the other hand if what is judged worthy of protection is not human life, nor yet living human tissue, but some fuller and richer description of just what it is that is morally significant about creatures like us, then we have to be more foxy.

The embryo is a fox

The foxy approach to the problem of the moral status of the embryo is more sophisticated. Typically the fox will attempt to identify morally relevant features of the embryo or fetus and argue that in virtue of its possession of these characteristics or capacities it is worthy of protection. The fox's virtue is its ingenuity so there are many different accounts that might be given of the moral importance of the embryo. The following is not untypical.

> By eighteen weeks the unborn child is a fully formed, unique human being, with all its major organs, apart from the lungs,

functioning. At this stage it is responsive to light, warmth, touch, sound and pain, and is even getting to know its mother's voice.[8]

The creature described in this passage, unique, fully formed, with all its major organs functioning, and sentient – responsive to light, pain, and so on – could be the normal adult member of a thousand or more species of creatures that inhabit this particular planet. Many millions of such creatures appear on the dining tables of those who would protect human embryos, and millions more are used for experimental purposes. The only justifications that can be produced for distinguishing morally between such fully formed, unique, sentient creatures and the human embryo[9] are either the bare and bleak stipulation that members of the human species are morally important and indeed superior *per se*; or, that the human embryo's moral importance lies not in what it is, but in what it has the *potential* to become.

Humans are the greatest

The belief that members of the human species are not only morally significant *per se*, but without a peradventure more morally important than any other creatures, is not without its attractions. Indeed we have the very highest authority for its respectability. Mary Warnock makes it a central plank of her own position. Speaking of preference for the human species she says:

> Far from being arbitrary it is a supremely important moral principle. If someone did *not* prefer to save a human rather than a dog or a fly we would think him in need of justification .... To live in a universe in which we were genuinely species indifferent would be impossible, or if not impossible, in the highest degree undesirable. I do not therefore regard a preference for humanity as 'arbitrary', nor do I see it as standing in need of further justification than that we ourselves are human.[10]

Repeating this thought more recently Mary Warnock has indicated that it was not only her own view but the unanimous view of the members of The Warnock Committee.[11]

Now of course it might plausibly be argued that to live in a universe in which we were genuinely species indifferent would be impossible or undesirable in the same sense as it might be impossible to be *genuinely* gender, race, religion, or nationality indifferent. But that does not mean that those with whom we do not share gender, race, or nationality are morally on a par with dogs or flies, or that we might defensibly so think of them. What makes racism or sexism wrong is not the simple fact that members of different races or genders are members of the same species but rather that there are no morally relevant differences between them.

Apart from its quite staggering complacency, we should be warned against the assertion that species preference stands in need of no further justification 'than that we ourselves are human', if only because the same impenetrable preference has been asserted for race, gender, and nationality with familiarly disastrous and unjustifiable consequences.

Potentiality

If the human embryo is not significantly different from other creatures, including the sunday roast, which we judge less morally significant, in terms of what it is (sentient, responsive and organs functioning, etc.) , except in terms of its membership of the human species, then we have no sufficient reason for according to it superior moral significance, unless we can show some other morally relevant feature. The one remaining candidate of any plausibility is its *potential*.

If we assume for the moment that normal adult human beings, creatures like you and me, are morally significant if anything is, then it is the potential of the embryo to grow into such a creature that distinguishes it from all other creatures and their embryos, including those destined to constitute the sunday roast. This argument has proved significantly attractive, as other chapters in this volume attest.[12]

There are two sorts of objections to the 'potentiality argument' for the moral significance of the embryo. The first is simply that the fact that an entity can undergo changes that will make it significantly different does not constitute a reason for treating it as if it had already undergone those changes. We are all potentially dead, but no-one supposes that this fact constitutes a reason for treating us as if we were already dead.

The second objection is simply that if the potentiality argument suggests that we have to regard as morally significant anything which has the potential to become a fully fledged human being and hence have some moral duty to protect and actualize all human potential, then we are in for a very exhausting time of it indeed. For it is not only the fertilized egg, the embryo, that is potentially a fully fledged adult. The egg and the sperm taken together but as yet ununited have the same potential as the fertilized egg. For something, or some things, have the potential to become a fertilized egg and whatever has the potential to become an embryo has whatever potential the embryo has.

Those who see in the potentiality argument the sole salvation of the embryo are quite naturally reluctant to accept the potentiality of the egg and sperm. They see a difference between the potential *of an individual* and the potential *to become an individual*. This distinction, if it identifies an important difference, makes it possible to regard the fertilized egg as a protected being without attaching any moral importance to the living human egg and the living human sperm which will become the embryo.

It is at this point that two sorts of defences of the embryo that we have thus far kept separate, unite in their susceptibility to a powerful objection. For both defenders of a preference for the human species as such and those who value human individuals for their potential to become the sort of beings that are morally significant – fully fledged adults – believe falsely that it is only the fertilized egg, the embryo, that qualifies. This is believed, so it would seem, because of acceptance of another false assumption, namely that it is only in the embryo that there is united in one place, in one individual, all that is necessary for continuous development to maturity.

This almost mystical reverence for the individual is never explained. Why is it right to protect individuals with the requisite potential but not pairs of individuals with the requisite potential? However, we do not need to press for an answer to this question because the possibility of parthenogenesis, both natural and artificially stimulated, puts paid to the idea that human individuals begin at or following conception.

Parthenogenesis

The eggs of most species, including humans, can be stimulated to grow without fertilization. This occurs naturally and randomly so far as we can ascertain, and may account for alleged examples of virgin birth, including that perhaps of Jesus – but only on the assumption that the son of the God of the Christians was in fact her *daughter*. For parthenogenesis only produces females. It is now possible to induce parthenogenetic growth of embryos grown *in vitro*. This possibility shows that the human egg is an individual member of the human species if the embryo is, for they both contain within the one individual all that is necessary for continuous growth to maturity under the right conditions.

Those who accept that we ought not to kill or use or experiment on individuals with the potential to grow into morally significant beings have then a substantial problem as to what to do about all those women who wantonly insist on consigning to their deaths every month the human individuals which they could so easily take steps to nurture and protect.[13]

Warnock on potentiality

Mary Warnock herself is ambivalent on the question of potentiality. The Warnock Report took the view that 'the objection to using human embryos in research is that each one is a potential human being'.[14] In a more recent essay Mary Warnock herself takes the view that 'The question whether or not they may be used for research must be answered not with regard to their potential, but with regard to what they are ...'. Indeed, she goes further, confirming the arguments above: 'To say that eggs and sperm cannot by themselves become human, but only if bound together, does not seem to me to differentiate them from the early embryo which by itself will not become human either, but will die unless it is implanted.'[15] Now with this, of course, I entirely concur. However, Warnock continues with a gloss upon how we are to understand 'what they are', namely as '... how far they are along the road to becoming fully human'.[16] But unless they are morally significant in terms of what they are at the particular moment at which the judgement is made, then this simply collapses into the potentiality argument again. For if what they are is simply beings a certain way along the road to becoming something else, namely fully human, then their status derives from their potential, not from their actuality.

Independent existence

There is a strong current of thought that attaches moral significance to the individual's ability to exist independently. For example, The Infant Life Preservation Act 1929 makes it an offence to abort or end the life of an individual capable of being born alive. The convention has been to regard 28 weeks as the point at which a fetus is deemed capable of being born alive and so abortions have to date been permitted up to that point. However, advances in neonatal care have steadily reduced this time until the fetus may with luck and high technology survive at 22 weeks. This has in part lead to pressure for a new Abortion Act, and the 'Alton Bill' recently considered by Parliament, but which failed for lack of parliamentary time, sought to reduce this cut-off point for permissible abortion to 18 weeks.

The ability to exist independently is a perplexing criterion. For one thing it makes the moral significance of the fetus turn on where it happens to be at the crucial moment. If its mother is near a major medical centre equipped to cope with premature babies, it might have a chance at 23 or 24 weeks. The further it happens to be from the premature baby unit the less its moral importance, until the wilderness swallows it up entirely. This approach makes moral importance not only geography-relative, but technology-dependent.

We may be on the verge of an era in which some embryos will be fertilized *in vitro* and will grow to maturity entirely independent of their genetic mother, nurtured in an artificial womb. Now of course this might be thought of as a form of dependence comparable to that on the mother, but only at the cost of regarding the equipment used to sustain premature babies in the same light, and equally, all the technology from pacemakers to dialysis which sustain the 'independent' life of so many adults.

The moral importance of the embryo cannot turn on something as slippery and as devoid of moral content as relative dependence.

Sentimental morality

One suggestion that has been influential is the idea that moral sentiments must play a crucial role in the determination of what is morally permissible. This idea, originating with David Hume, has been influential in the work of a number of contemporary moral philosophers.[17] In particular, Mary Warnock has made it a central part of her own approach to these issues. It generates a strong and a weak thesis and we must be clear about both of these possibilities.

Briefly, the idea is:

> If morality is to exist at all, either privately or publicly, there must be some things which, regardless of consequence, *should not be done*, some barriers which should not be passed.
>
> What marks out these barriers is often a sense of outrage, if something is done; a feeling that to permit some practice would be indecent or part of the collapse of civilisation.[18]

As I say, this idea generates a strong and a weak thesis. The strong thesis is, that, where people's moral sentiments are outraged at the very idea of something, this fact *of itself* shows that what outrages them contravenes morality. The weak thesis on the other hand is that wise legislators will regard public sentiment as strong evidence about the morality of those expressing the sentiment and will therefore try not to violate or disregard these moral beliefs.

Mary Warnock herself seems to vacillate between these two, sometimes seeming to support the strong thesis and at other times the weak. For instance in her introduction to the Blackwell's edition of The Warnock Report[19] she adopts the strong thesis, using it as a form of veto. She argues that only if the advantages of embryo experimentation in utilitarian terms 'seemed very great' and *only if*[20] 'there were no absolute outrage of general moral sentiment', should the embryo be used for research. However, in her more recent essay she suggests that the role sentiment plays is not so much that of a sort of veto or test that actions or practices must pass if they are to be permissible, but more an exercise in political compromise ... 'of attempting to come up with a moral solution to problems which, while retaining as many of the calculated benefits as possible, will nevertheless offend and horrify people as little as possible'.

Both the strong and weak forms of this thesis suffer from the same fundamental weakness, which is that they both assume that a sense of outrage is always a sense of *moral* outrage. While I myself think that David Hume's remark, quoted with approval by Warnock,[22] that morality is 'more properly felt than judg'd of', is just plain wrong, and indeed that the converse is nearer the truth, even those who are inclined to accept it must face the problem of how to determine when one's feelings are moral feelings and when they are not.

This is a point of quite fundamental importance. For we can recognize that we ought, if we can, to respect people's moral beliefs or feelings even where we disagree with them (I say 'if we can', because we might not be able to do so without compromising our own moral beliefs). We can see that it is this belief, that we ought to respect the morality of others, which makes the weak thesis very attractive indeed, for it is one formal way of expressing our respect for morality itself.

But the crucial problem entirely ignored by Warnock is that not all feelings are moral feelings and not all outrage is moral outrage. So that while we ought to respect the moral beliefs and feelings of others even where we don't share them, we have no reason to respect their prejudices or brute preferences or aversions. Not only are we under no obligation to respect such things – they are not respectable. If we look at Mary Warnock's own elaboration of her idea we can see clearly why this must be so.

> Someone who feels that, for example, to shovel the dead into the ground without ceremony is wrong, may be able to say no more than that he regards such practices as unfitting or unseemly or uncivilised. But these very sentiments give rise to imperatives: one *must* treat the dead with respect. Similarly, ... those who object ... to commercial agencies for the supply of surrogate mothers may feel simply that they would be ashamed to live in a society where such agencies were permitted. To have such a feeling of shame must lie at the root of any moral principle.[23]

Now it is not impossible that such feelings lie at the root of any moral principle. But such feelings also lie at the root of many immoral principles and brute prejudices. We know of so many analogous feelings: that women are innately inferior and it is unseemly and unfitting for them to indulge in many 'male' occupations, or to appear in public unless swathed from head to toe; that many people have felt ashamed to live in a society that permitted marriage between members of different 'races', or in which public institutions and places of resort were not racially segregated; or in which homosexuality was treated other than as 'a vice so abominable that its mere presence is an offence'.[24]

The first duty of someone who thinks that morality matters is to examine his/her feelings to attempt to see how and to what extent they cohere with his/her principles, whether they are simple personal aversions interesting only to the extent to which we are interested in the biography of the person whose feelings they are. And the first duty of those who are trying to determine public policy is to try to distinguish between expressions of outraged prejudice and expressions of outraged moral feelings. For even the weak thesis does not require us to respect bigotry, however passionately felt.

The moral sentimentalist[25] owes us an account of how to identify moral feelings and distinguish them from prejudices.[26] For unless s/he provides this, deference to moral feelings is indistinguishable from deference to prejudice and the moral imperatives generated by sentimental morality are in effect injunctions to ignore moral reasoning altogether.

In order to know what bearing public sentiment is to have on the question of the moral status of the embryo, we need to know something about the grounds of the beliefs of which the sentiment is the expression. Now of course if nothing turns on the outcome, then there is no reason not to give way even to prejudice. If everyone feels, for whatever reason, that the dead should always be buried with ceremony, then if there's no reason not to do so this should certainly be permitted. However, there is seldom so unequivocally neutral an expression of public sentiment and it is time to remind ourselves of what reasons we might have for permitting the use of embryos for research and as sources of cells and tissues.

Why experiment on embryos?

There can be few people who do not know the role that research using human embryos has played in the treatment of infertility and in evolution of the techniques that have made so-called 'test-tube' babies possible and which have helped so many couples to have the children that they so passionately want. Less well publicized are the possibilities that are opening up of using embryo research for diagnostic and therapeutic purposes.

In vitro fertilization offers the possibility of indentifying genetic abnormalities in the embryo *before* implanting it into the uterus. As Robert Edwards has noted:

> the 'abortion *in vitro*' of a defective preimplantation embryo ... would be infinitely preferable to abortion *in vivo* at twenty weeks of pregnancy or thereabouts as the results of amniocentesis are obtained. It would be less traumatic for parents and doctor to type several embryos and replace or store those that are normal rather than having the threat of a mid-term abortion looming over each successive pregnancy.[27]

The same technique will permit the determination of the gender of each embryo, with the consequent possibility of screening effectively for sex-linked genetic disorders. There are also very good indications that embryo or fetal cells, tissue, and organs can be used for repair and transplants in adults. These techniques may make possible the repair of inherited enzyme defects, the treatment of diabetes using pancreatic cells, and embryonic myocardial tissue could be obtained from embryos and used by cardiologists to repair the major vessels of the heart.[28]

In his chapter in this volume, Robert Edwards reports[29] that work is far advanced on mouse embryos which if repeated in the human embryo will provide a good chance of repairing radiation damage of the sort caused at Chernobyl.

It has recently been reported elsewhere[30] that tissue from the brain of an aborted human embryo of around nine to twelve weeks' gestation has been used in the treatment of Parkinson's disease.

While it is not clear precisely which lines of research will be most useful, nor what other promising possibilities will arise in the future, we do know that none of them is likely to be realized without embryo research. If, as seems overwhelmingly probable, embryos can be used to save the lives of adults and children and for therapeutic and diagnostic purposes, we would require strong moral arguments indeed to justify cutting ourselves off from these benefits, with the consequent loss of life and perpetuation of pain and misery. Before returning to the question of whether such arguments are available we must pause to consider whether morally relevant distinctions can be made between embryos.

Spare embryos

There are two different sources for embryos or indeed fetuses that might be used for research or therapeutic purposes. The first are those grown externally in the laboratory. These may not all have been conceived *in vitro*, for the process called *lavage* is a way of recovering from the mother not eggs, but early embryos which have been fertilized *in vivo* not *in vitro*. However, all these are early embryos and they all end up growing *in vitro*, wherever they started out, so I shall for convenience call them IVF embryos. The second source are embryos or fetuses, usually at a much later stage of gestation, which are the products of abortion.

Now among IVF embryos we need to make three further distinctions. There are those healthy embryos which have been grown with a view to implantation in a mother with the hope that they will grow into normal adult human individuals. These may be 'fresh' growing in the laboratory or frozen for future implantation. The second group of embryos are those which are sometimes called 'spare' embryos. The hormone treatment which produces excessive or 'superovulation' in women so that a number of eggs can be recovered at a time, may lead to the existence of embryos which are spare in the sense of being more than are required for implantation either presently or in the future. These spare embryos may be normal or anomalous. Those with anomalies of any sort – possible defects which might prevent normal development – would not be implanted. Normal spare embryos are suitable for implantation but are superfluous to requirements. The common feature of all the embryos so far discussed is that they have been produced as part of a programme designed to result in embryos for implantation. Finally there are what have sometimes been called *research embryos*. These are not produced with a view to implantation but are gathered for research purposes only. The usual source for these embryos are women who wish to be sterilized and who are asked if they are prepared to donate eggs for research. These eggs are then fertilized and the resulting embryos constitute the so-called *research embryos*.

Robert Edwards[31] draws a firm distinction between using spare embryos and using research embryos, arguing that there is something degrading about producing embryos at will merely for research purposes. He believes it permissible to use only those spare embryos that are anomalous in some way and that would consequently be unsuitable for implantation in any event. There are three possible interpretations of this unease. One focuses upon the moral character of the researchers, arguing that those who would deliberately choose to create embryos for their own purposes alone are somehow morally deficient. The second is a form of Warnockian argument, suggesting that the feeling that one would not wish to live in a society that permitted such feelings is of itself evidence of its immorality. And third there is an oblique reference to the potentiality argument, the suggestion being that anomalous embryos are not even potential human individuals and so there can be no harm in using them, whereas normal embryos should be implanted and given their chance to develop.

The first two interpretations are good reasons for Professor Edwards to refrain from doing things that make him uneasy. The question is, though, whether others who do not feel as he does should refrain on these grounds? The only difference between using spare embryos and using research embryos that we have not already considered is the *intention* of those who produce them. Spare embryos are produced in order to establish a successful pregnancy and research embryos are produced in order to do research or to provide sources of tissue or cells for beneficial use in others. There is no difference in the moral status of the respective embryos, nor is there any difference in what will actually happen to them. The difference is only in the initial intention behind their production. I cannot but think that if it is right to use embryos for research then it is right to produce them for research. And if it is not right to use them for research, then they should not be used even if they are not deliberately created for the purpose.

If, as is believed, the 'cost' of producing a live birth by normal sexual intercourse is statistically the loss of three embryos in early miscarriage or failure to implant, and it is not wrong knowingly to attempt to have children at such a cost, then it is not wrong to attempt to save the lives of other adults at the same or a comparable cost.

A similar feeling of unease sometimes attends the use of material from aborted fetuses. Reports that such material is being used to treat Parkinson's disease, for example, have met with opposition.[32] This seems to be a straightforward example of cadaver transplants. It is true that the fetus cannot consent to its cadaver being used for transplants but then there is no question of its withholding consent either. It is not the sort of being whose own consent can be relevant one way or the other, for it is not capable of forming a view about the matter. So long as the mother of the embryos consents, then the situation is entirely parallel with other cadaver transplants, from children for example, and there are no peculiar ethical issues which need special consideration.[33]

The moral status of the embryo

We must return finally to the question of the moral status of the embryo. We have seen that this cannot be determined by its potential, by what the embryo will become, but must be assessed in terms of what it is. I have set out in detail elsewhere my own arguments about the criteria for moral significance of the individual and my answer to the question of when and in virtue of what embryos might begin to matter morally.[34] I argue that the moral status of the embryo and indeed of any individual is determined by its possession of those features which make normal adult human individuals morally more important than sheep or goats or embryos. Now, while I have a positive account of what these features are, I do not need to deploy it here. For it is clear that *at no stage of its development* does the human embryo nor yet the human fetus possess these characteristics. This was clear in our consideration of 'foxy' arguments about the status of the embryo.

Thus, while I think that at no stage of its development through to the end of the third trimester of gestation and beyond does the developing human individual acquire those features that make its moral significance comparable to that of normal adult human beings – that in short make it a person, we do not need to set out here the criteria for personhood. The reason is that there are no grounds for distinguishing the criteria appropriate for the legitimacy of research on embryos from the criteria for legitimate abortion. So that all and any envisaged research on embryos or use of embryonic tissue for therapy could be permitted and would be permissible on the same terms as permissible abortions.

The reason is easy to appreciate. It is that any society which considers that the preservation of the health and wellbeing of its members constitutes grounds for abortion should take precisely the same view of research on, and use of, embryos for precisely the same reasons. Between 150,000 and 170,000 abortions are performed annually in the United Kingdom alone. The embryos and fetuses thus lost are seldom of beneficial use to society. I cannot imagine what moral argument would support the legitimacy of abortion on the grounds that it is necessary for the health and wellbeing of the mothers concerned, and yet would not support embryo experiments which would preserve the lives and promote the health of present and future individuals.

The crucial issues seems to be this: we have no reason to think that the embryo, nor yet the fetus, attains a moral status comparable to that of adults at any stage of its three trimesters of gestation, whether these occur in the womb or not. The changes that occur in the developing embryo, while real and fascinating, do not make for important moral differences. At no stage does the embryo or the fetus become a creature which possesses capacities or characteristics different in any morally significant way from other animals or mammals. It differs from other creatures to be sure in its membership of the human species and in its potential for development to human maturity. But in these respects it does not differ from the unfertilized egg.

When we bear in mind that, as Robert Edwards has argued in this volume, most of the secrets of the development of life are contained in early embryos, and that we are extremely likely to be able to use what we learn from such embryos to save many lives and ameliorate many conditions which make life miserable, we would not only be crazy but wicked to cut ourselves off from these benefits unless there are the most compelling of moral reasons so to do. I have argued that there are no such compelling reasons.

Notes

1. Robyn Rowland, 'Making women visible in the embryo experimentation debate', *Biotechnics* 1.2 (April 1987) 179.
2. Lady Warnock prefers the title 'chairman'.
3. Mary Warnock, 'Do human cells have rights?', *Bioethics* 1.1 (January 1987).
4. ibid. p. 1.
5. John Harris, '*In vitro* fertilization: the ethical isues', *The Philosophical Quarterly* 33 (1983) 217–37.
6. Isaiah Berlin, *The Hedgehog and the Fox* (London: Weidenfeld, 1967).
7. H. W. Jones Jnr, 'The ethics of *in vitro* fertilization – 1981', in Edwards and Purdy, eds, *Human Conception* In Vitro (London: Academic Press, 1981).
8. Society For The Protection Of The Unborn Child leaflet entitled 'Back The Alton Bill', January 1988.
9. For brevity I shall often use the terms 'embryo' and 'fetus' as equivalents.
10. Mary Warnock, '*In vitro* fertilization: The ethical issues II', *The Philosophical Quarterly* 33 (1983) 238.
11. Warnock (1987) p. 10.
12. See John Marshall's chapter in this volume, pp. 55–64.
13. I am assuming here the moral equivalence of acts and omissions. I have argued for this equivalence at length elsewhere, in my *Violence and Responsibility* (London: Routledge & Kegan Paul, 1980), and see for example: *The Value of Life* (London: Routledge & Kegan Paul, 1985) Ch. 2.
14. *The Report of the Committee of Inquiry into Human Fertilization and Embryology* (London: HMSO, July 1984) – The Warnock Report, S. 11. 22. p. 66.
15. Warnock (1987) p. 8.
16. ibid.
17. David Hume in his *A Treatise of Human Nature* (1738). Contemporary philosophers with a similar approach include Stuart Hampshire: see for example his *Morality and Pessimism* – The Leslie Stephen Lecture (Cambridge: Cambridge University Press, 1972) and Bernard Williams in, for example, his *Against Utilitarianism*, in B. Williams and J. J. C.

Smart, *Utilitarianism For and Against* (Cambridge: Cambridge University Press, 1973).

18 Warnock (1987) p. 8.
19 Mary Warnock, *A Question of Life* (Oxford: Basil Blackwell, 1984) p. xv.
20 My italics.
21 Warnock (1987) p. 8.
22 ibid.
23 ibid. pp. 8 and 9.
24 Devlin, *The Enforcement of Morals* (London: OUP, 1959). I am indebted here to Ronald Dworkin's critique of Devlin in his *Taking Rights Seriously* (London: Duckworth, 1977) Ch. 10.
25 In another context I called this approach to ethics 'olfactory moral philosophy', in deference to some remarks of George Orwell on the importance of using one's nose when thinking about right and wrong. See *Violence and Responsibility* (1980) Ch. 7.
26 Ronald Dworkin shows one way of doing this. See Dworkin, op. cit.
27 Edwards and Purdy, eds, *Human Conception* In Vitro (London: Academic Press, 1981) p. 373.
28 ibid. p. 381.
29 See this volume, p. 50.
30 This was anticipated in 1981. See Edwards and Purdy, op. cit., pp. 373ff. The use of embryonic tissue is important because whereas human brain cells do not regenerate in adults, they do in embryos and if embryo cells are transplanted into adults these cells may continue to grow and may stimulate adult cells to regenerate also. Such use of fetal material in the UK was first attempted in Birmingham in April 1988.
31 See this volume, p. 49.
32 See, for example, *Medical Monitor* 26 (January 1988) 1.
33 It seems clear that the benefits from cadaver transplants are so great, and the reasons for objecting merely selfish or superstitious, that we should move to mandatory cadaver transplants and remove the habit of seeking the consent of either the deceased or relatives altogether, as we already do when *post mortem* examinations are ordered without any consents being required.
34 See Harris, *The Value of Life* (London: Routledge & Kegan Paul, 1985) Ch. 1.

Chapter six

At Heaven's command?: the Churches, theology, and experiments on embryos

Anthony Dyson

The principal Churches in Britain today are making a substantial, well-informed, and timely contribution to the public debate about different aspects of bioethics.[1] In this chapter I do not offer fully orchestrated theological arguments for and against experimentation on human embryos. Rather, I want to examine in some detail the sources to which appeal is made in these Church statements, how the relationship between these sources is understood, and what processes of moral reasoning are implied by the responsible use of these sources. I shall conclude from this analysis that the issue of experimentation in theological ethics is much more open than some people suppose.

After drawing briefly on Gill's recent book *Beyond Decline*, part of which raises quizzical questions about Church pronouncements, I examine the main sources which are appealed to in these statements.[2] I go on to suggest that underlying different permutations of these sources are fundamental differences betweeen precritical and critical views of theological knowledge. However, following Gilkey, I judge that the contrast between these two approaches is, in consequence of recent profound changes in our culture, no longer that which the eighteenth-century Enlightenment bequeathed to us. This new situation calls for an attitude towards scientific and technological culture which is both affirmative *and* critical.

Next, I discuss two of the central sources in theological ethics, namely the Bible and Natural Law. Among other things, the use of these two sources often lacks adequate linkage with empirical Knowledge and with Experience. Neither source, alone or in combination, can be appealed to *directly to settle* contemporary bioethical problems. In looking specifically at experimentation on human embryos, I put forward for consideration three topics: the appeal to interdependent as well as to individual experience; the claims of posterity; and the centrality of risk, tragedy, and sacrifice.

In Chapter Two of his recent book *Beyond Decline*, under the title of 'The Gulf in Social Pronouncements', Robin Gill observes that

> most church assemblies and synods today feel the need to make pronouncements upon a range of moral and social issues. Even though they are fully aware that their role in society is more marginal than it might have been before their current state of decline, they still feel this need.[3]

This appears unexceptionable. A Church, believing that a truth which comes from God is being challenged, expresses itself in public, whether to mould public opinion, to persuade others to alter legislation, to play the role of the prophet who discerns the signs of the times, or from another worthy motive. But in fact Gill continues in a way which may surprise the reader:

> some commentators have even contended that this felt need [to make pronouncements] is actually a symptom of decline. As churches decline and become more marginal in a pluralist society so they seek to compensate by taking specific positions on moral and social issues.[4]

In this manner, Gill begins his exercise in *critical suspicion* about a phenomenon which may have initially seemed perfectly simple and straightforward..

I do not propose to take Gill's own analysis much further, though towards the end of my discussion I shall touch upon one aspect of it again. Instead, taking Gill's exercise of critical suspicion as my starting-point, and in a way which complements Gill's own argument, I want first to note the principal types of moral reasoning which are used by the Churches at the present time in the bioethical field. These types can be characterized by reference to which source or sources are judged to be authoritative. In the moral reasoning of the Church pronouncements some or all of the following sources of authority are invoked in different orders of precedence and in different permutations: Scripture, Tradition, Natural Law, (empirical) Knowledge, Experience, and Reason. (Throughout the chapter I shall capitalize the first letter of each of these terms, except when they appear in a quotation uncapitalized.)

Scripture, i.e., the Christian Bible, means the canons of Old and New Testament, with or without the Apocrypha. We should take note of the substantial distance between those who treat the Bible (or parts of it) as *itself* authoritative 'revelation', and those who see the Bible as a more or less direct witness *to* 'revelation' which has taken place in the history of the peoples and cultures from which it comes.

Tradition can mean the body of revelation handed to the apostles and prophets. It can refer to a body of teaching handed on orally. It can mean the truth of the gospel transmitted from generation to generation in and by the Church. It may simply refer to an individual Church practice or custom. The meaning of the term usually intended in this chapter is 'the accumulation of the wisdom of the Churches' past'.[5]

Natural Law is a much disputed concept, as will become clear later in this chapter. Most agree that it stands independently of revelation and is accessible to human reason. One definition runs: 'the law implanted in nature by the Creator which rational creatures can discern by the light of natural reason.'[6] But this definition harbours some problems.

By *Knowledge* is meant, in the present context, the up-to-date body of information and theory produced by the natural and human sciences through a wide variety of intellectual activities.

The appeal to *Experience* is to the direct life-experience of individuals and groups or, more narrowly, to religious experience as part of experience as a whole. I shall use it here in both senses.

The term *Reason* occurs in theology and philosophy in many different senses. For some it has meant a faculty which, illuminated by God, can penetrate to divine truth. In this chapter I shall use it to refer to the employment of the mind in rational ways, proceeding on its own authority.

Now it will be clear even from these preliminary definitional remarks that these terms, which crop up so widely and frequently in the theological discussion, have a wide range of related meanings, are very unspecific in character, and may overlap each other to some extent. These characteristics will become even more apparent when I turn to look at the usages of the different Churches.

Some consideration of the use of the six sources to which the Church statements appeal can be found in the document *Public Statements on Moral Issues*.[7] It includes sections outlining the ethical and theological methods used in, and the moral authority claimed for, public utterances by the Church of England, the Free Churches, the British Council of Churches and the Roman Catholic Church. I shall discuss the first two and the last of these.

In the case of the Church of England it is said that 'Anglican moral reasoning assumes both the legitimacy of the use of reason in interpreting Scripture and Tradition, and the need to take adequate account of the results of empirical investigation'.[8] Further, Anglican moral statements 'represent, not magisterial declarations totally confined to the terms of a moral tradition, but the product of grappling with new questions in the light of that tradition, and in the process developing it further'.[9] Within this kind of approach one point should be especially noted: 'if the Church has anything to offer from its own theological and moral tradition, it will make its contribution as it studies the facts of the matter, interpreted by those who are professionally occupied with them'.[10] This point is amplified thus: 'moral statements prepared within the Church of England attach considerable significance to the ethical judgements and practice of those professionally engaged with the matter under enquiry, and to the development of professional practice'.[11]

The section of the report which deals with the Roman Catholic Church begins by referring to a claimed authority in moral statements different from the claims made by the Church of England and the Free Churches: '... the Roman Catholic Church claims authority to interpret divine Revelation, which in its turn is considered to illuminate and enrich natural law'.[12] It follows from this that 'the authority attaching to the Spirit-enlightened source of a magisterial statement ... is "no less" a motive for acceptance than the arguments contained in the statement.'[13] This is a very important qualification which will be discussed later in this chapter. But, granted this proviso, 'Roman Catholic moral statements argue their case by appealing strongly to Scripture, to patristic teaching, to previous authoritative magisterial statements, to the Church's tradition and to human reason'[14], what is involved in this appeal to Reason? 'Arguments from reason occasionally adduce anticipated harmful consequences ... but for the most part they appeal to obligations considered to derive immediately from human nature as created and redeemed within the salvific plan of a provident God.'[15] This dense passage appears to be saying that the use of reason is not to be taken normally to refer to, for example, the active execution of a utilitarian calculus; instead, reason articulates the content of a call to obedient response to the teachings of Natural Law seen in the light of the gospel. Reason is not employed to break new ground.

In the case of the Free Churches, 'all would assert that the Bible has a particular authority in matters of Christian faith and practice'.[16]

> Whatever is understood to be the teaching of the whole of Scripture is bound to be formative of Free Church thought. Negatively any statement that could be shown to be in contradiction to what is taken to be the teaching of the Bible would not be understood as a Christian statement. When appropriate, appeal is made to Scripture concerning those matters that are within the direct compass of Scripture.[17]

But 'along with the Bible the tradition of the Church's teaching has its own authority'.[18] However, such tradition is never received uncritically. 'The Christian response to a particular issue may itself change and develop.'[19] This Free Church statement allows that new moral issues, or old moral issues under reconsideration, are not resolved simply by quoting the Bible or by referring to the tradition of the church. For 'empirical evidence carries its own weight and is an important factor in the process of making moral decisions'.[20] In sum, 'Free Church statements ... related to the Bible, the tradition of the Church's teaching, contemporary experience and the necessary empirical evidence'.[21]

Some general conclusions of *Public Statements on Moral Issues* can be elicited at this point since they will bear upon the later discussion. All agree in principle on the importance of the Bible. But in the Roman Catholic (RC) usage, anything said about the Bible must be related to the claim about the 'Spirit-enlightened source of a magisterial statement'. The Free Church (FC) position makes important qualifications about the use of the Bible. 'The teaching of the *whole* of Scripture' carries most weight. Anything contrary to the teaching of the Bible would not be part of a Christian statement. But FC plainly allows that there are ethical matters *not* within the compass of Scripture. The Church of England (CE) and FC lay most stress upon the problems of new ethical issues and upon the flexibility required to respond to them. Perhaps, therefore, it is not surprising that CE and FC appeal to empirical evidence in the way that they do. CE gives weight to what may be called the *ad hoc* nature of its mode of enquiry and in particular of its seemingly tentative theological practice, e.g. '*if* the Church has anything to offer from its own theological and moral tradition, it will make its contribution *as it studies* the facts of the matter ... '.[22] RC, by contrast, sets its ethical judgements in the context not so much of the empirical evidence, but rather 'in the context of a more positive and general theological and philosophical treatment of the subject'.[23] CE and FC are apparently more open to consequentialist argument than RC. RC alone of the three refers directly to Natural Law.

From this limited analysis of *Public Statements on Moral Issues*, it is nonetheless possible to discern some of the major methodological difficulties which attend the Churches' forays into social ethics in general and into bioethics in particular. As soon as we begin to explore these difficulties, it quickly becomes apparent that we are dealing with fundamental theological questions about the nature and self-revelation of God, and about the relation of God to the world of nature and history. For present purposes, we can adopt in a preliminary way Fritz Buri's articulation of the basic methodological problem.[24] Should the tradition have priority over the understanding, or should the understanding have priority over the tradition? Buri's formulation carries within it an opposition between a pre-critical and a critical view of knowledge. In the *pre-critical* theological perspective, humans are obedient and deferential to what is given, towards the objective salvation-history which has been created and managed for them, with its crucial moments in the history of the old, and in the beginning of the new, Israel. In the *critical* mode, humans exercise suspicion towards what is given, not least towards the monuments of the past, for all historical and scientific judgements are only judgements of probability. The world is recognized as, at least in part, a human-historical construction, the product of the successful shouldering of distinctively human responsibility. But the critical mode, which has been formidably in evidence since the eighteenth-century European Enlightenment, in so comprehensively calling into question the absolutizing tendencies of the pre-critical mode, runs the risk of absolutizing itself.

A general account of the macro-movements of recent and contemporary culture has been undertaken by Gilkey in his essay on 'Theological frontiers'.[25] He has important things to say about the setting in which a theological contribution to bioethics must operate. Gilkey speaks first of the

old frontier ... the challenge issued to theology by the Enlightenment; that whole cultural-historical development of new this-worldly and optimistic attitudes, new methods of inquiry, new critiques of traditional authorities, new moral and social aims and standards, and, perhaps most important, new criteria for truth.[26]

The consequences of the old frontier were what we now term 'modern culture'. Among the theological responses to this new culture engendered by the Enlightenment have been

the reinterpretation of the *cognitive* claims of theology and of the status and character of religious truth in the face of natural science, social science, and modern philosophy ... and ... the re-interpretation of theology in the face of historical change, and hence of the *historical* relativity of every theological expression whether in scripture or in tradition....[27]

Gilkey goes on to make the exceedingly important point that *neither the sciences nor medicine have experienced this old frontier*. He says that 'the intellectual culture of the West, at least its academic culture, still reflects Enlightenment and post-Enlightenment perspectives on all these issues, especially on the unambiguous status of science and its praxis'.[28] Not surprisingly, theology and ethics, the laying of whose foundations antedates the old frontier era, have experienced in the old frontier era a 'somewhat one-sided set of relations to biology, genetics, psychotherapy, and medicine'.[29]

But, argues Gilkey, the old frontier, which we call 'modern culture', is now itself under threat. For 'much is new here':

the [post-Enlightenment] secular culture was overwhelmingly strong, confident, and irresistible – and religion and ethics unneeded, in theoretical disarray and internally confused. Now it is the secular culture that primarily finds itself threatened, by internal uncertainty and self-doubt and by forceful external criticism.[30]

It is not surprising therefore, that ... many in our age seek renewed religion, ethical guidance and renewal, and that many more tend to lose their faith in our established forms of cognitive inquiry and of social authority.[31]

Gilkey is clear that this state of affairs constitutes an opportunity for theology and ethics. But theology's and ethics' response to this new frontier must not be a primitive restorationism. For the character of society in the new frontier must be recognized as irreducibly and inescapably that of an *advanced scientific* and *technological* culture'. 'Science and technology are now essential to the contemporary life and well-being of the culture; they *must* be there or the culture will die.'[32]

If we take this picture as representing with some degree of accuracy the transitional period in which we find ourselves, what consequences does this have for the theological-ethical method? I shall argue in the remainder of this chapter that the theological ethicist must, on the one hand, eschew excessive intellectual capitulation to the mores of the 'old frontier' culture of the nineteenth century and beyond, but without failing to take account of the lessons learned. But, on the other hand, there is no going back behind the old frontier in the sense that we could, or really might even want to, turn our backs upon the advanced scientific and technological culture which is ineluctably and necessarily our destiny for as far ahead as we can see. What has this to say in particular for two of the sources of authority upon which many of the Churches' ethical claims have rested, namely Natural Law and the Bible?

The concept of Natural Law was the amalgam of different strands of thought by the time of Aquinas. Some of these strands were somewhat contradictory. One saw Natural Law as a more exalted notion of justice than human justice; another saw it as a blind inner force of nature. One saw Natural Law as closely linked to revelation; another kept the two firmly apart. In Aquinas, however, Natural Law is neither law in the sense of human laws, nor is it law which derives from revelation. Instead Natural Law is connected with the moral presupposition upon which all human laws depend. If this is the case, it is clearly quite mistaken to entertain hopes that straightforward rules for human living can be 'read off' from Natural Law. There are indeed norms written into human nature, but these are only realized after much careful and many-sided reflection as a consequence of which certain insights begin to emerge about what 'being human' means. It is now apparent why Natural Law cannot be equated with 'laws of nature'. For Natural Law is not directly based on, nor directly perceptible from, the world which humans share with other biological phenomena. Rather it is concerned with the interpretations which we evolve out of our recognition of our experience of the distinctively human. We have, therefore, to exercise great care in attempting to move from the 'primary recognitions' to specific rules. We may not move from a general biological good, for example, to such statements as 'you must not use artificial birth-control'. The correct kind of move would come in the form of saying 'some arrangements should be made ... for the organization of the family'.[33]

Granted that Natural Law theory has some strengths, which include its universality and its role in reminding us of the moral challenges which we constantly face and to which we as constantly turn a blind eye, we have to avoid giving the impression that Natural Law is unchanged and unchanging. In fact, the more Natural Law descends from the heights of abstraction, the more disagreement and debate about correct interpretation is legitimate and necessary. So Natural Law is to be seen as a human construct which will vary from age to age. It does not primarily appeal to what is natural in human life but rather centres upon what is constructed by interpretation. It is quite mistaken, therefore, to suggest that Natural Law is in principle opposed to science and technology. It cannot be invoked to support a primitivist credo.

What effect does a misunderstood Natural Law theory have upon the other sources to which ethics appeals? Three important observations can be made.

First, when Natural Law is invoked as an unchanging and unchallengeable body of ethical law, there arises a tendency to say that the content of Tradition is none other than Natural Law. When an abstract Natural Law theory thus impinges upon Tradition, the effect is for the latter to lose its historical and existential, diverse and dynamic, character, and to become ahistorical, monolithic, apparently uniform in all times and places, invulnerable to criticism and revision.

Second, we have observed how Natural Law has become fatally

confused with 'laws of nature'. One result of this has been to make Natural Law too 'physicalist' (as some writers put it) in character. This is particularly noticeable in the application of Natural Law theory to matters of sexuality and reproduction, where a criterion of *biological* teleology has been very much in evidence at the expense of the psychological, existential, and personal dimensions of humanhood.

Third, perhaps the most sinister feature of a misconceived Natural Law theory comes into view when the open moral discussion, upon which the interpretation of the *humanum* depends, is by-passed. A proposition is then accepted or rejected, not on the cogency or otherwise of the argument, but as a requirement demanded by some kind of magisterial authority. (This phenomenon can be seen in the statements of the Roman Catholic Church, but it is in fact not confined to that Church.) When this demand is made, a difficulty is encountered. For exponents of Natural Law theory, even in its most conservative form, would agree that the precepts of Natural Law are rational in character and are therefore, in principle, open to some measure at least of rational verification or falsification. Hence those who appeal to Natural Law should be willing to furnish grounds or warrants on which the Natural Law precept is based. From which areas might those grounds or warrants be derived? Primarily these would be derived from Knowledge and Experience according to the definition of these terms set out above.

A well-known instance of conflict in the use of Natural Law surrounds the papal encyclical *Humanae Vitae* (1968).[34] A small Pontifical Study Commission on Family, Population and Birth Problems, convened by John XXIII, first met in 1963. It was enlarged by Paul VI in 1964 to include experts from moral theology, reproductive biology, medicine, demography, economics, sociology, and pastoral care among its fifty-eight members. This Commission reported to Paul VI in mid-1966. The majority view was that contraception was not intrinsically evil. Paul VI's response in *Human Vitae* two years later rejected the Commission's majority report and reaffirmed traditional Roman Catholic teaching on artificial contraception. I do not want to argue for or against the teaching of *Humanae Vitae*, but rather to note its method. Hellegers has observed that the encyclical lacks any reference to 'scientific evidence for, or indeed of scientific thought in reaching, the conclusions which the encyclical draws'. Again, the encyclical 'nowhere acknowledges that there might have been new biological facts of importance since the encyclical *Casti Connubii*' of 1930. Hellegers goes on to note that, for the encyclical, 'nothing that a present or future scientist could possibly contribute in terms of scientific data could have any pertinence to the subject'. Thus he observes that it 'implies that theology need not take into account scientific data, but shall reach its conclusions regardless of present or future facts'.[35] The encyclical affirms Natural Law theory but the reader is left to take it on trust that all the reasons which have led to a negative conclusion have been rehearsed; they do not appear in the text. In this case, therefore, the principle of the appeal to Knowledge breaks down.

Natural Law is, as we have seen, in part an appeal to personal Experience; not to the episodic and varied experiences of isolated individuals, but to an appreciable body of consistent Experience which, in one sphere or another, helps to identify and advance the characteristically human. As an example of appealing to Experience in this way, we can point to the Lambeth Conference's statements on the same subject as *Humanae Vitae* discussed above. Prior to the 1958 Conference, the mind of the Lambeth fathers had been against artificial contraception, though its views had tempered somewhat since the beginning of the century. The 1958 Conference had before it an important study-document on *The Family in Contemporary Society* which rehearsed the demographic, philosophical and theological arguments.[36] But the study-document also introduced an argument from Experience.

> It is stated, and stated truly, that to many saintly people the thought of contraception is so repugnant as to argue a radical incompatibility between those practices and the development of holiness of character.... This argument deserves serious attention If the testimony of those most advanced in that life is against any practice, that is a very weighty argument against its moral-ity.... But in the case before us, this testimony is far from being unanimous enough to provide a simple solution of our problem. One knows other Christians, not less advanced in holiness (so far as one can judge in these matters), who have no such 'instincts'. How is one to judge between them? Only if there are independent arguments which convince us in favour of the one or the other.[37]

In the actual Report of the 1958 Conference, the study-document's more tentative appeal to Experience is given considerably more weight. The Conference in a sense puts into the form of a Resolution a moral judgement already made for years before by Christian husbands and wives, episcopal, clerical, and lay, who had admitted contraception into their married life and could not convict themselves of sin for having done so. The moral claim implicit in that behaviour, once recognized, proved a powerful factor in an ethical change of mind being arrived at, in the event, very quickly.[38]

So, both *Humanae Vitae* and Lambeth 1958 are case-studies for the contribution of Knowledge and Experience to the human construction of Natural Law. But we have also seen how ambiguous these appeals to Knowledge and Experience can be. The papal Commission which ultimately led to *Humanae Vitae* produced a majority and a minority report. The Lambeth study-document noted a group to whom artificial contraception was repugnant and a group to whom it was not. On what basis does one make a judgement, especially if the person or body making the judgement has no capacity to arbitrate between conflicting scientific opinions?

A further problematic feature of the appeal to Experience can be framed in the question, 'To *whose* Experience are we to appeal?'. From where does the individual theologian or corporate assembly draw upon personal Experience as a source of authority? This question also leads us to enquire about the way in which Experience contributes to the formation of Tradition. Where is Tradition found and to whom does it belong? This question then leads to further questions as to who exercises power over whom.

Two examples will suffice to establish these points. First, most of the decision-making as to what counts as 'valid' Experience and 'valid' Tradition is in the hands of Church leaders and their civil service. A favourite topic for church statements is sexuality and sexual behaviour. Now historical study in recent decades has succeeded in partly lifting the veil from a number of hidden histories in the realm of sexuality. For example, feminist ecclesiastical historiography has shown beyond dispute that over long periods of time women's experience in this area (and in most other areas too) has been ignored in the construction of patterns of Experience. Second, Boswell's study of the history of homosexuality in the Church shows that, whatever may have been the 'official' tradition, there were quite different traditions in some parts of the Church which greatly qualify what is meant when we refer to 'the Church's condemnation of homosexuality'.[39] Thus we see how, from the side of Natual Law, the content of Tradition can be abstracted and generalized so that it becomes less receptive of the variety of Experience, especially if all or part of that Experience belongs to the powerless.

Following this discussion of Natural Law, I now turn to the second topic for more extended discussion, namely the use of the Bible. I distinguish (and oversimplify) here between a 'traditional' or pre-critical, and a 'modern' or critical approach. The traditional approach, despite its many forms, is identified by its common conviction, namely that the text of the Bible is *itself* revelatory. The critical view, in contrast, sees the Bible as, in various ways, a *witness to* revelation in nature and history.

On the *traditional* approach, the preferred procedure is to find a text or texts which seem to give an explicit ruling on the issue under discussion. If this is not forthcoming, a second procedure is to find a text or texts which give a more general ruling. If this is not forthcoming, a third procedure is to search for a broad theme, common to the whole of the Bible, which pertains to the issue under discussion.

It seems as if the first procedure, seeking an explicit text or text, would be the most rewarding; but it is also the most open to rebuttal by historical or other critical methods. (See, for example, the critical problems of the New Testament texts on marriage and divorce.) The second procedure, namely the search for texts offering more general rulings, is less open to immediate rebuttal and to the charge of being relative only to its own culture. But it requires a deductive process before a ruling can embrace the specific issue. It is then more open to the citing of exceptions. The third procedure, in which the exegete hunts for the 'Biblical view' of *x, y,* or *z,* although it is attractive to the traditional exponent who has intellectual reservations about the first and second procedures, falls down because it is so general and, more seriously, because the Biblical writings are so varied that it is exceptionally difficult to come up with *the* 'Biblical view' of anything, unless one trims the evidence.

In fact, all three procedures which try to move directly from the text to the exegete and back, underplay the setting-in-culture of the texts. But the users of these texts will want to claim that they do decisively *settle* the issues under discussion, because, *a priori,* the users believe that God has plainly revealed God's ethical demands in the text of the Bible. This makes it clear why the users undoubtedly prefer the first procedure which, as we shall see, gets them into all sorts of exegetical tight corners.

A *critical* approach, on the other hand, regards the Biblical writings as of human making, springing from a variety of eras and cultures, and as witnessing in a variety of ways to what the authors and compilers, with the communities to which they belonged, believed about the character and demands of God. Here the authority does not rest in the Biblical writings as such. They cannot *settle* anything for *us.* Indeed, on some matters they might lead us grievously astray, e.g. by the patriarchal attitudes in parts of the Bible or by the anti-semitism in the Gospels. What the Biblical writings can offer is a way-in to a rich, complex, and ethically-charged body of experience, of memory and hope, stamped, as far as the New Testament is concerned, with the marks of the destiny of Jesus of Nazareth. It follows that the Christian Churches have every justification for including all or part of the Biblical writings among the sources of authority which are drawn upon to make ethical judgements today. Problems arise, however, when commentators attempt to impose the traditional theory of Biblical authority upon the Biblical writings as a way of dealing with issues in bioethics. I shall examine an example of this approach. It concerns the *status of the conceptus*, which is of course a much disputed issue in the matter of experiments on embryos.

The Bible contains no systematic discussion of the status of the conceptus. This should not be regarded as a criticism of the Biblical writings, for they are not the kinds of literary genres in which one might expect to find discussions of that nature. But clearly there are many contemporary Christians who believe that the Bible establishes and/or confirms that the conceptus is from the 'moment' or, better, from the 'process of fertilization', a unique human being.

A thoughtful attempt to find Biblical texts which might be held to bear directly upon this question has been made by David Atkinson.[40] It is not possible to present a full account of his arguments; a sample must suffice – namely some discussion of Psalm 139. This psalm includes the passage:

> You created every part of me;/ you put me together in my mother's womb./ I praise you because you are to be feared;/ All you do is strange and wonderful./ I know it with all my heart./ When my bones were being formed,/ carefully put together in my mother's womb,/ when I was growing there in secret,/ you knew that I was there –/ you saw me before I was born. (vv. 13–16a).

I want to comment on the two 'general conclusions' to which Atkinson comes about this psalm. I take them in reverse order. First, Atkinson writes,

> to put the argument at its weakest; even if we have to be agnostic about the appropriateness of calling every early conceptus a 'person' ... Psalm 139 makes clear in some cases at least (such as this psalmist) there is a continuity of personal identity from conception to maturity.

A few lines earlier Atkinson was arguing, not on theological grounds, but presumably on scientific grounds, that 'through all the various discontinuities of development, there is this continuity of organic integration which marks the continuing identity of the conceptus, embryo, foetus, child and adult'.[41] What is added to that statement, which is presumably an empirical statement open to falsification and verification, by Atkinson's words which I quoted, 'Psalm 139 makes clear that ...'? Surely the psalmist is using religious, poetic language to emphasize God's reliability and providential care in relation to humanity. The language is not factual language; nor can it prove or disprove factual assertions.

The second of Atkinson's two 'general conclusions' actually makes the point which I have just made: '... the poetic power of the psalms depends on the generalizations which we make. We are involved in the psalms. Their words stand as testimonies very often not just to the truth about one individual, but about human life before God.'[42] Here Atkinson correctly recognizes that the meaning of the text emerges from a mutual hermeneutical encounter between text and interpreter. But that meaning is existential-religious, not empirical. Again, following Torrance and others, Atkinson argues that the virginal conception of Jesus allows us to say, as a corollary, that 'the divine Son of God has joined himself with human flesh precisely at the point of conception'. Atkinson comments: 'The word has become flesh, *so to speak*, right down to the level of our genes'.[43]

Torrance's main argument appears to correlate a religious-theological statement with a factual statement by simple identification. But Atkinson's words 'so to speak' seem to pull back from the brink of a confusion of categories. Nonetheless, Atkinson proceeds to other arguments which make the same kind of dubious correlation. He argues from the Greek word *brephos* (which in classical Greek is used for both embryo and child) that its use in different contexts (Luke 1.41: 2.12,16; 18.25) leads to the conclusion that 'some sort of continuity is implied linking embryo, child in the womb, new-born baby and infant'. The interpretation reaches an extraordinary point when Atkinson discusses the visit of Mary to Elizabeth (Luke 1.39f). Elizabeth, six months pregnant, calls Mary 'the mother of my Lord'. Here, only ten days after Mary has conceived, she is called a mother. Atkinson goes on: 'And then the fetal Messiah is recognised by the six-month old fetus, the still-to-be-born John the Baptist, jumping with joy in Elizabeth's womb!'.[44] It is not at all clear what kind of discourse is in use here, but clearly this sort of language cannot be held to add to our empirical knowledge of conception and gestation.

In my discussion of Atkinson I have (to do him the best justice possible) accepted without question the authenticity of the Lukan texts as in some sense themselves revelatory, as embodying themselves a divinely intentioned meaning. In fact, historical-critical scholarship would deal with these texts in a way which cannot sustain that kind of direct interpretation at all.

What conclusions can we draw about the use of the Biblical writings in bioethics? I have suggested that authoritative rulings on particular issues are not available and that to cajole such rulings from the Bible is to do it a disservice. But earlier in this chapter I mentioned two other interpretative procedures. These were the appeal to more general rules from which the more specific rule can be inferred, and the appeal to pan-Biblical themes. The first of these is important. For the reference to more general rules keeps the challenge of good versus evil before people's eyes. To that extent it has much in common with the primary precepts of Natural Law. But if we take a more general ruling which has a close bearing on the subject of this essay, namely 'thou shalt not kill' we must note that it almost certainly means 'thou shalt not murder', and also that the Biblical writings allow important exceptions to the rule. So, just as in the case of Natural Law, a lot of work remains to be done in using the Bible in relation to today's bioethical issues. The approach via pan-Biblical themes is not any more helpful (even assuming it is feasible) since these turn out also to be very general in character.

The oddness of these kinds of use of the Biblical writings becomes evident when we observe how the theologian presents Biblical norms, rules, and laws which have no reference, immediate or distant, to the central figure of the Christian cultus, creed, and community – namely Jesus of Nazareth. In a general sense, the centrality of that person would seem to oblige those who see themselves in some kind of relationship to Christianity to come to the use of the Bible with an 'essence of Christianity' *already* in mind. And that 'essence of Christianity' should surely include at its centre direct or indirect reference to the lived destiny of Jesus of Nazareth, that is, to what is believed about him expressed in the religious symbols of 'life, death and resurrection'. I shall return to this perspective in the final section of this chapter.

In the light of the foregoing discussion of the sources utilized in the church statements, especially the Bible and Natural Law, I want to focus, under three headings, upon the interrelationships between the different sources.

First, there is little doubt that in practice many applications of Natural Law theory make their moral rulings on the basis of Natural Law, confirmed by Scripture and Tradition, with little or no reference to Knowledge and Experience. An example comes from a recent Roman Catholic *Instruction* which includes judgements on experimentation with embryos.

> From the time that the ovum is fertilized, a new life is begun which is neither that of the father nor that of the mother: it is rather the life of a new human being with his (*sic*) own growth.... This teaching *remains* valid and is further confirmed, if *confirmation were needed*, by recent findings of human biological science.[45]

Here an ethical conclusion is reached without any *necessary* reference to Knowledge and/or Experience.

Second, another example comes from the large amount of time and effort which is being expended by the churches in discussing the ethics of homosexuality.[46] Scientifically, the aetiology of homosexuality is uncertain and disputed. Any 'Knowledge' in this area is extremely tentative. The Biblical references (even assuming it is proper to quarry for ethical statements in that way), if they are in fact references, are at the least hotly contested. Tradition at the level of the Churches' social history still contains gaps of substance and interpretation. Imaginative literature and personal witness on the experience of homosexuality is rarely introduced into the discussion. Yet in this complex and volatile situation, various degrees of condemnation come forth from the Churches and from individual theologians. Some assert that the condition of homosexuality is not sinful but its practice is. If this is the case, what kind of activities are condemned? Some say that only anal intercourse is condemned. If so, is female homosexual practice not condemned at all? Are there, *mutatis mutandis*, aspects of heterosexual practice which ought to be condemned? These and other kinds of ethical improvisations on right and wrong do scant justice to the factual and moral complexity of heterosexuality and homosexuality. Further, it has to be borne in mind that the discussion is taking place in a culture which has been discriminatory and hostile to homosexuality, so that, however unbiased a contemporary interpreter may be supposed to be, it is difficult to escape, at some level of consciousness, attitudes which predispose the interpreter negatively. In these circumstances there seems to be a strong case for working out what would be involved in an official moratorium on formal ethical statements about homosexuality, with a simultaneous commitment to other modes of enquiry which would directly or indirectly foster a better appreciation of what the main sources of moral reasoning have to offer today!

Third, there is another, more comprehensive sense in which Experience bears in a special way upon Scripture, Tradition, Natural Law, and Knowledge. There is no doubt that in many Church pronouncements the appeal to Experience is muted. There is more than one reason for this. One factor may be that, since the Churches are hierarchically structured and dominated by a body of clergy or laity (or both), not much effort has been made to ascertain what the experience of the many could contribute to the decision-making of the few. In one respect this could be particularly important. Many of the bioethical issues impinge directly or indirectly on sexuality and reproduction. Many of the (usually male) judgements in these areas have been arrived at without any or much reference to the experience and contribution of women. The feminist movement has rightly had a good deal to say about the theory and practice of that studiously nonchalant approach to the experience of women.[47]

I want now to relate the foregoing discussions more directly to the question of experimentation on human embryos. I shall look at this issue in relation to the Bible, Tradition, Experience, Knowledge, and Reason.

First, it must be conceded that the Biblical writings do not yield any direct or specific information about the status of the embryo. Indeed, to put this question to those kinds of sources is probably a mistake in itself. If we look instead at Biblical themes, then the constantly recurring theme of divine creation has to be reckoned with. Certainly the doctrine of creation implies the need for respect towards human life. There is an ethical presumption against killing, though with important exceptions. But it does not follow that human life is to be regarded as sacred or holy. In the Judaeo-Christian tradition, God alone is sacred and holy. The created order is material, subject to finitude and evanescent. On the status of the embryo the Biblical writings only serve the ethical debate in a general way.

Second, from early in the Tradition, a distinction was drawn between an 'unformed' or 'formed' fetus. This distinction was based on whether or not the fetus could be recognized as 'human'. Using ideas from Aristotle, this distinction came to be developed to embrace a notion of 'progressive ensoulment', i.e. from a vegetable soul via an animal soul to a human soul. The fetus was regarded as 'formed' when it was physically developed enough to be the recipient of a human 'soul', namely forty days for the male and eighty days for the female.

From the seventeenth century the opinion began to gain ground that the soul was present from conception. In 1869 Pius IX took this view as germane to his critique of abortion. In the traditional view, the killing of both the unformed and the formed fetus was judged to be sinful, though only the killing of the formed fetus was deemed to be murder. At the present time the official Roman Catholic standpoint seems to be that human life begins at conception, though it is a philosophically open question whether ensoulment takes place then or a little later, say at implantation; but to be on the safe side it will be assumed that ensoulment takes place at conception.

Objections to this position can be made from a number of directions. I want to make the more radical and less common point that, theologically, the notion of the 'soul' is problematic, based as it is on a sharp dualism between body and soul. The Roman Catholic standpoint in a sense endorses that dualism when it insists that questions about the soul are beyond scientific competence. If it is preferable to use the notion of 'personality' instead, then what has been thought of as 'soul' becomes the *raison d'être* of the whole process of growth and individuation – the hominization – of the embryo. On this account, the question as to the sense in which the embryo is a human being would require empirical judgements about the embryo's emergent recognizability as a person. This position seems much closer to the tradition of progressive ensoulment in the earlier tradition. Thus the possibility of research and the type of research would here depend upon what was proposed to be done at what stage.

Third, in considering Experience in relation to experiments on embryos, it is important to look critically at the tradition of theological and philosophical 'individualism' in the West. Of course there is much in that tradition for which we can be grateful in terms of human rights and freedoms, and of safeguards against the constant threat of extremes of collectivism with their neglect of individual conscience. But the rise of an individualism which had religious and theological, as well as social and political aspects, whilst rightly opposing all forms of totalitarianism, also obscured the notion of human *interdependence* with its constant dialectic between self and self, self and selves, selves and selves, self and whole, and selves and whole. I shall mention two examples of the presence and absence of Experience in these respects.

1. In a pioneering article, Stendahl has convincingly shown that much traditional interpretation of the apostle Paul's theology has been based on a mistake. Typically, many interpreters since the period of late medieval piety, including Luther, have interpreted Paul on conscience and the law, and thus effectively on justification (salvation), in terms of the individual's inner, spiritual, existential life. But, writes Stendahl, 'it appears that Paul's reference to the impossibility of fulfilling the Law is part of a theological and theoretical scriptural argument about the relation between Jews and Gentiles'. Again,

> Paul had not arrived at his view of the Law by testing and pondering its effect upon his conscience; it was his grappling with the question about the place of the Gentiles in the Church and in the plan of God ... which had driven him to that interpretation of the Law which was to become his in a unique way.[48]

Here, I should simply wish to register the possibility of saying that the ethical 'unit' is not the individual as such; it is not a case of individuals being justified one by one. It is the empirical, interdependent community which is justified. Indeed, on this view of things and taking up a theme from Mathers, the individual cannot be fully justified (saved) until all (the interdependent community) are and is justified.[49] If this line of theological reasoning is pursued, then perhaps (and I put the argument in its weakest form) the judgement about experimentation must be as much directed to the destiny of the interdependent human community as to that of the individual.

2. In what may be called 'first phase' feminism, a strong attack was directed upon patriarchy which kept a woman in exclusive relationship with a man, and with the nuclear family, thus withdrawing women from a network of woman-to-woman relationships in which they felt at home and within which feelings, gifts, and responsibilities were shared. It is no surprise therefore that Christian feminist writers who seek to construct a non-sexist doctrine of humanity inclusive of women and men, should lay so much emphasis upon their human 'bonding' as against the 'diremptive' impulse of patriarchal man.[50] This sort of outlook reflects how in points of view thrown up by the feminist debate many women tend not to want to regard their child, their body, their life, as exactly a private possession. They express an interest in more open-textured patterns of family life. Many women (and it is to be said that feminism is understandably divided on these matters), including those who are not self-conscious feminists, seem relaxed about, and see no ethical problem in, donating ova to other infertile women or in making the use of their womb available in a surrogacy arrangement. It is not a case of what a woman shall give away and what retain of her 'possessions'. This kind of legal vocabulary which appeals to the language of property-ownership is probably inherited from medieval doctrines of the marriage contract and of men's rights, though in its context that legal provision did much for women in subjecting arbitrary behaviour by men to the rule of law. This broader and more open-textured approach to relationships, which has become evident out of the critique of sexism in the period of the 'old frontier', obviously converges to some extent upon the notion of interdependency in the apostle Paul as noted above.

Fourth, what role can the authority of Knowledge play in formulating a point of view which does not rule out the ethical possibility of experimentations on human embryos? I want to look at this in two time-perspectives: in relation to the past and in relation to the future.

1. In *Public Statements on Moral Issues*, the Free Churches allowed that some moral issues were not within the compass of the Bible.[51] What kind of Knowledge lies beyond the compass of the Bible? It is not simply that computers and nuclear weapons are not mentioned

in the Biblical writings. The greater difficulty for us occurs where contemporary possibilities and choices take us beyond the *range* and *kind* of those found in the Bible. It is one thing to rule on the case of a pregnant woman caught up involuntarily in a male brawl so that she loses her child by the injuries caused to her;[52] it is a different thing to remove ova from a woman, with her consent, for them to be used after IVF for research into miscarriage. I am not here arguing that the latter procedure is thereby justified; it is more complex than that. The judgement of this second act is of a kind other than that of the first, involving as it does intentions, circumstances, consequences, capacities, and Knowledge of a different order than anything found in the Biblical writings. There is no neat and tidy way of going directly to and from the Bible in this kind of ethical issue. So the past cannot serve the present in any immediate way.

2. In thinking about experimentation on embryos we are concerned with another time-perspective – namely posterity. One of the crucial arguments in favour of experimentation is that there is reasonable confidence that considerable benefit may come from work on, e.g. identification of genetic and chromosomal disorders, miscarriage, contraception, etc. But there is apparently a great gulf fixed between supportive, therapeutic, and altruistic acts from one person to another, and relationships with yet-to-be-born, abstract posterity. In fact the stimulus towards a personal self-relating attitude to posterity has in modern times come not from Christianity but from ecology. Christianity has often showed itself less than kindly disposed towards the perspective of posterity. Most of early Christianity looked for an imminent Second Coming. When that End did not come, it was relocated in two other contexts. Either the End was achieved in and through the institutionality of the Church as a holy society separate from the world and an earnest of the future heavenly city and/or the End was relocated in an eternal, transcendent realm above. With these two relocations, the sense of urgency of the original eschatological hope was largely lost. The recent rediscovery by ecology of an urgent future, and the recognition of causal links between our actions and the wellbeing, even survival, of posterity makes much more concrete the reality of the future human community. Thus the love-ethic may now have to be seen as relevant not only to the individual/corporate neighbour at hand, but also to the neighbour in the future with whom we are linked by ecological filaments. The discovered human future now becomes a principle by which to correct the interpretation of the Biblical writings and Tradition, and so help the emergence of values from these sources which are pertinent to that urgent future. So, the responsible experimentation on human embryos in relation to defined goals

might begin to acquire the shape of an act of neighbour-love towards the future human community.

Fifth, I remarked near the beginning of this chapter that Reason stood somewhat apart from the other sources of authority with which I would deal. For Reason has to be used to handle all these other sources. One major shift in the operation of Reason and of the character of our 'epistemological environment' must be mentioned here. As Dewart observes:

> the most primitive fact in the Hellenic-Western epistemological tradition is the dichotomy of self and non-self.... *Every* being confronts *every other* being; for insofar as anything is a being, it is self-contained and distinct ... from the rest of the universe. On this view 'to be acquainted with reality is not to interact with it.... It is not, for instance, to converse with it.'[53]

But in one of the most significant changes in human self-consciousness, we have begun to see ourselves as participating in the act of knowing; the observer becomes part of the reality. Much of the early ethical tradition of the Christian West was based on the former view. In theological ethics that tradition was content to have God, the Bible, or the Church as the source of ethical laws to which the appropriate response was heteronomous obedience. But analogous with the philosophical view of knowing in which the human being is participant, so in theological ethics the key-word for this involvement by the human being is *responsibility*.

In this chapter I have tried to develop an account of what might be involved in taking responsibility for the use of the several sources of moral authority where *the givenness of the moral order is not ready-to-hand but has to be painfully constructed out of the interplay of those sources*. Using this approach, I have come to the conclusion that the bases of argument in some of the attempts to anathematize experiments on human embryos are unsound, and that there is the possibility, on the other hand, of handling these several sources in a creative way that does not rule out such experimentation as unethical, and may even support its use under certain conditions and in certain circumstances. But I do not want simply to replace one assertive argument by another. My introduction of 'interdependence' and 'posterity', for example, though they point to a different and positive theological approach, can no more *settle* definitively the ethical issues in experimentation on human embryos than the arguments against experimentation can. For as we have seen, the sources of authority are many, admit of many permutations, and are each and all in constant flux as Knowledge and Experience change, and as the Bible, Tradition, and Natural Law are criticized and so criticize us afresh. The work of theologians and of the Churches, faced by the challenge of radically new steps in experiments, does not lie in the issuing of incontestable statements. A better way in Church pronouncements which helps people to be themselves fully involved in the continuing moral search, and which helps them to live creatively with moral inconclusiveness, is urgently needed.

If, as I believe, the ethical dilemma surounding embryo experimentation is so delicate and unstraightforward, how does it come about that so many Christian adherents pronounce so confidently against experimentation? One small part of a large answer can be mentioned – taking up another of Gill's points in *Beyond Decline*.[54] It might be argued that the case of those who defend the total, or near-total, inviolability of the embryo/fetus, and who thus do not recognize there to be any ethical dilemma, as well as expressing their conscientious conviction, it also part of a broader phenomenon. Since we still live in part in the 'old frontier', where the sacred is still engaged in fierce confrontation with the secular realm, and where (it is said), more and more, Christian beliefs and ideals are being surrendered to the secular invasion, where the Churches retreat slowly but inexorably through prepared position to prepared position, is there not an overwhelming compulsion to identify *one* position (and it cannot be 'God'; for 'God' in our society is publicly dead) at which the believers can stand firm and which the opponents cannot seize? Thus the coming together of sperm and ovum is maintained as a point of indecipherable mystery, overriding any kind of scientific account and any kind of theological or philosophical objections.

But the possibility (as I have argued) that a different case can be reasonably, faithfully and plausibly made out with a responsible attitude to the sources of authority, does not mean that experimentation can ever be lightly undertaken. If the irreducible 'essence of Christianity', which cannot exclude the lived historical destiny of Jesus of Nazareth, is marked by, among other things, pain, risk, and tragedy, then we cannot be surprised if in proceeding with such experimentation – with the best regulation and legislation – the deepest questions about the meaning of human life are touched upon, and the sense of loss, as well as of gain, found to be inescapable. Nonetheless this is not in itself an argument in favour of staying one's hand.

Notes

1 See bibliography in Kevin T. Kelly, *Life and Love: Towards a Christian*

Dialogue on Bioethical Questions (London: Collins, 1987) pp. 157f.

2 Robin Gill, *Beyond Decline: a Challenge to the Churches* (London: SCM Press, 1988).

3 Gill, *Beyond Decline*, p. 20.

4 Gill, *Beyond Decline*, p. 20.

5 See Hans-Georg Link (ed.), *Apostolic Faith Today: a Handbook for Study* (Geneva: World Council of Churches, 1985) pp. 79–83.

6 Art., 'Natural Law' in F. L. Cross and E. A. Livingstone (eds), *The Oxford Dictionary of the Christian Church* (London: Oxford University Press, 1974) p. 956.

7 British Council of Churches, *Public Statements on Moral Issues: A Report from the Liaison Committee of the British Council of Churches and the Roman Catholic Church in England and Wales* (London and Abbots Langley: British Council of Churches and Catholic Information Services, n.d.).

8 BCC, *Public Statements*, p. 11.

9 BCC, *Public Statements*, p. 9.

10 BCC, *Public Statements*, p. 9. This is a quotation from the 1965 Report *Abortion: an Ethical Discussion*.

11 BCC, *Public Statements*, p. 9. This section of the Report, judging by its style and sentiments, is the work of Professor Gordon Dunstan. He has influenced the form and matter of many Anglican reports along these lines; but others do manifest a different approach.

12 BCC, *Public Statements*, p. 22.

13 BCC, *Public Statements*, p. 22.

14 BCC, *Public Statements*, p. 22.

15 BCC, *Public Statements*, pp. 22f.

16 BCC, *Public Statements*, p. 13.

17 BCC, *Public Statements*, p. 13.

18 BCC, *Public Statements*, p. 13.

19 BCC, *Public Statements*, p. 14.

20 BCC, *Public Statements*, p. 14.

21 BCC, *Public Statements*, p. 14.

22 BCC, *Public Statements*, p. 9 (my italics).

23 BCC, *Public Statements*, p. 23.

24 Quoted in A. O. Dyson, *Who is Jesus Christ?* (London: SCM Press, 1969) p. 120.

25 Langdon Gilkey, 'Theological frontiers: implications for bioethics', in Earl E. Shelp (ed.), *Theology and Bioethics: Exploring the Foundations and Frontiers* (Dordrecht: D. Reidel Publishing Company, 1985) pp. 115–33.

26 Gilkey, 'Frontiers', p. 116.

27 Gilkey, 'Frontiers', pp. 116f.

28 Gilkey, 'Frontiers', p. 118.

29 Gilkey, 'Frontiers', p. 117.

30 Gilkey, 'Frontiers', p. 120.

31 Gilkey, 'Frontiers', p. 121.

32 Gilkey, 'Frontiers', p. 121.

33 Some of the critical discussion in this section is indebted to Columba Ryan, OP, 'The traditional concept of natural law: an interpretation', in Illtud Evans, OP (ed.), *Light on the Natural Law* (London: Burns and Oates, 1965) pp. 13–37.

34 *On Human Life, Encyclical Letter of Pope Paul VI* (Humanae Vitae) (London: Catholic Truth Society, revised edn, 1970).

35 Quoted in LeRoy Walters, 'Religion and the renaissance of medical ethics in the United States: 1965–1975' in Earl E. Shelp (ed.), *Theology and Bioethics*, pp. 9f.

36 *The Family in Contemporary Society* (London: SPCK, 1958). Also in Ian T. Ramsey (ed.), *Christian Ethics and Contemporary Philosophy* (London: SCM Press, 1966) pp. 340–81 (extract only).

37 Ramsey (ed.), *Christian Ethics*, p. 372.

38 G. R. Dunstan, *The Artifice of Ethics* (London: SCM Press, 1974) p. 48.

39 John Boswell, *Christianity, Social Tolerance and Homosexuality: Gay People in Western Europe from the Beginning of the Christian Era to the Fourteenth Century* (Chicago: University of Chicago Press, 1980). See also John Boswell's pamphlet *Rediscovering Gay History: Archetypes of Gay Love in Christian History* (London: Gay Christian Movement, 1982).

40 David Atkinson, 'Some theological perspectives on the human embryo (part 2)', *Ethics and Medicine: A Christian Perspective* 2.2 (1986) 23f, 32.

41 Atkinson, 'Some theological perspectives', p. 23.

42 Atkinson, 'Some theological perspectives', p. 23.

43 Atkinson, 'Some theological perspectives', pp. 23ff.

44 Atkinson, 'Some theological perspectives', p. 24.

45 Congregation for the Doctrine of the Faith, *Instruction on Respect for Human Life in its Origin and on the Dignity of Procreation* (London: Catholic Truth Society, 1987) p. 13 (my italics).

46 E.g. General Synod of the Church of England Board for Social Responsibility, *Homosexual Relationships* (London: Church Information Office, 1979).

47 See Beverly Wildung Harrison, *Making the Connections: Essays in Feminist Social Ethics* (Boston: Beacon Press, 1985).

48 Krister Stendahl, 'The Apostle Paul and the introspective conscience of the West', *Harvard Theological Review* 56 (1963) pp. 199–215.

49 See A. O. Dyson, '"What, after all, is health?": James Mathers as critical pastoral theologian' in *Pastoral Studies Spring Conference 1987* (Birmingham: Department of Theology, Birmingham University, 1987) *passim*.

50 See, e.g., Margaret A. Farley, 'New patterns of relationship: beginnings of a moral revolution', *Theological Studies* (1975) pp. 627ff.

51 BCC, *Public Statements*, p. 13.

52 See Exodus 21, 22.

53 Leslie Dewart, *The Foundations of Belief* (London: Burns and Oates, 1969) pp. 76, 62.

54 See Gill, *Beyond Decline*, p. 21.

Chapter seven

An irresolvable dispute?

Keith Ward

In this chapter I shall discuss mainly the philosophical and ethical issues which the topic of experimentation on embryos raises. I shall also advert to some theological issues, but not primarily. I shall select four areas where I think there are very basic philosophical disputes of what I would take to be an irresolvable nature. I would call each of these areas essentially contestable areas, intending by that to mean that there is no agreed method of resolving any disputes in these areas. That may already sound as if I am taking a position; it is not meant to. It is meant to be a dispassionate statement of the facts. However, such statements appear to be impossible in this context and already I have distanced myself from a view which would say that human reason on its own can work out the answer to this problem. It is not just that some people are stupid, or cussed, or ignorant. It is because of very deep philosophical disputes that there is no prospect of agreement. What is to be done about that I will discuss at the end of the chapter.

The first issue that I will talk about is the issue of verificationism. This is an important issue, though it is primarily a philosophical one. It is a topic in epistemology, in how it is that we can come to know anything, and the verificationist view is that there must be ways of getting agreement at least on all factual matters by observation. There is a weaker view which would allow the use of arguments as well; but I am dealing here with a rather stronger view that on all factual matters, by observation, there are ways of getting agreement. So, if you are looking at embryos and ask the question, 'Are these things persons or not?', all the *facts* about embryos are known and very few of them are disputed. There are no hidden facts to find out. We know all the observations that we could make and everybody agrees about them. If there is anything left over after that, it can't be a factual matter. And that, I think, is partly why The Warnock Committee didn't raise the question explicitly of when is something a person, because at least some of the Committee took the view that

that is not a factual question, for you get the facts by looking at what you can observe through microscopes, etc.

Thus, whether you call a small embryo a person or not is a matter of convention; it is a matter of your decision. And it is primarily a moral decision when you say (if you do say), 'It is a person'; what you are saying is 'I will not permit this entity to be destroyed'. You might put that by saying it has a negative right to life – a negative right meaning that everyone has a duty not to kill it. Of course small embryos don't have all human rights; they don't have the rights to holidays with pay, for example. But the one right you may think they do have is the right not to be killed, which means that everyone else has a duty not to kill them. However, the question of when something has got this right is a matter of decision. On a verificationist view, it is up to you to decide. It is not a factual issue at all; the question 'Is an embryo a person?' may sound like a factual question, but it is not. It is a disguised moral question and perhaps the disguise is rather misleading, causing you to think that there must be some hidden facts which you could find out if only you looked a little harder. Of course decisions about whether killing embryos is permitted or not can be more or less reasonable. You can produce arguments for them. It is not that it is all completely irrational, that reason doesn't work; but for a verificationist it is not a factual issue.

There is of course an alternative view. Verificationism does not hold the field even in its most sophisticated forms. There are people who would very strongly deny it as a philosophical position. The chief opponent of a verificationist view would be someone like Richard Swinburne (but not only he), who might say that observations of things that you can see through microscopes are certainly relevant to knowing whether or not something is a person. Nevertheless the question 'Is it a person?' is not a question to be answered solely by empirical observation. For a person is a kind of thing, and 'kinds of thing' are such that we sometimes have to infer from evidence whether or not they exist.

There are questions which have answers which are either true or false, but of which it is not possible to *establish* the truth or falsity. I shall give an example from a slightly different but relevant field. Suppose I ask the question 'Do lobsters feel pain as you put them into pans of water and they appear to scream?'. That is a factual question, it seems; it is a question about whether lobsters feel pain. It certainly sounds factual – not just a question of decision – and yet of course there is no way of resolving the question. Some people in my experience would say, 'That's not a scream; it is wind escaping'. Other people will say, 'Yes, it is very like a scream to me and I am sure that they are feeling pain'. However, it appears to be a factual question – whether they feel pain or not – and yet it is not susceptible of definite, conclusive, overwhelmingly obvious resolution. There is no way of getting all rational observers who know all the empirical facts to agree about this. So that is one example of a non-verifiable statement of fact. Another one is 'Is an embryo a person?'. It is not verifiable. There is no way of getting everybody to agree about it. Nevertheless it is a factual question. The thing either is a person or it is not, and it is up to you to produce evidence for whether it is a person or not.

I will suggest now a definition of what a person would be, consistent with this view. It is not enough to say that a person is just what actually and obviously exists at this moment and can be observed to exist. For example, I am not just a person if I am writing at this moment and if I stop writing I am not a person any more. Again, you cannot say that persons are things which speak rationally, assuming that that is happening, and that if I stop speaking rationally I am no longer a person. If I go to sleep you don't say I have stopped being a person. If you give me an anaesthetic and I become unconscious I don't stop being a person. So it is not enough to say that a person is something which is actually indulging in some rational activity. What can we say? I will propose a formula which is the best I can think of in this area, namely that a person is an entity of a kind to which it is proper to ascribe a number of specified attributes – let's call them rational attributes. I shall spell out a little of what I mean by saying this.

First, you don't find out what a person is by looking very hard at a particular instance of a person. You don't look, for example, at a mentally subnormal human being and say 'Is this a person? Is it exhibiting rational properties? Is it behaving in rational ways?'. You do not ask the question 'Is this actual entity behaving rationally or is it capable of behaving rationally?'. You rather ask 'Is it a member of the class of things which behave rationally?'. This is a way of getting over the problem of how you classify mentally subnormal or senile or very young people; you can say they are members of a class of things which have rational abilities even if they don't have them themselves. That is what is important, that they are members of that class. So you would probably want to say (if you held this view) that in fact the class in question is simply the class of human beings, and it is therefore sufficient to being a person that you are a human being. You are a kind of entity to which it is proper to be rational and you don't ask specific questions about whether *you* are rational or not.

You can see why Jewish philosophers in particular, the Chief Rabbi for example, feel very strongly about this. For once you start setting criteria for being a person then he, the Chief Rabbi, will remember a time in history when he didn't qualify. Anybody who has been through such an experience and has been classified as a non-person fit for destruction, will be very wary about drawing up lists of which people are actually exhibiting personal properties.

So you can see why we might want to go to a wider view and say, 'Let's not ask whether I fit; do I have an IQ of 140?; is that high enough to be a person, a rational agent?'. Maybe I don't want to ask that sort of question. I just want to say 'Look, I am a human being at least and if I am a human being then that is a kind of thing to which it is proper to have rational attributes'. So you would be talking about *natural kinds* of things. That view is very different from the verificationist's. Verificationists would say that they could not see any of these natural kinds: if a thing is a natural kind, that is a matter of decision. The natural kinds theorist would say it is not a matter of decision; it is a matter of truth.

Of course, in a funny sort of a way you have to make a decision about whether it is true or not – but it is still a funny sort of decision because what you have to do is think about all the evidence and the arguments for or against, and you will find the belief forming in your mind. You don't actually choose the belief. The natural kinds theorist will say it is neither true that I choose it to be the case that x is a person, nor is it true that I choose to believe that x is a person. What I can choose is to look at all the relevant evidence and the arguments in their context and then, without my choosing, I will come to have a belief of a certain sort, which is a belief about a fact that such and such is a person. The question at issue is this: 'Is this embryo a member of the natural kind, the class of things, to which it is proper to possess rational attributes?' Observations are evidence for that, but they don't conclusively give an answer. There is still a sort of decision to be made.

That is the first issue on which you are going to get a dispute between people who say they are only going to consider the actual behaviour and the observable facts about persons that we can see. Looking at embryos, we can say that they don't behave much like rational agents and they certainly don't exhibit any rational qualities. So the answer will almost inevitably be for a verificationist that an embryo is not a person. For the natural kinds theorist, it doesn't matter whether the embryo exhibits rational capacities and abilities or not, because the question is, 'Is it a member of the kind of thing to which it is proper to possess rational attributes?'. And the answer would probably tend to be 'Yes' in that case, because it simply is a little human being, as far as one can tell. That is one contested view on which we have already to make a decision – not a moral decision, I might say. It is a decision about what our most general descriptions of the natural world are to be. It is a very fundamental, philosophical dispute.

The second issue that I want to discuss is in fact the issue of personal identity. Here again I am oversimplifying by only giving two alternatives in each case, but for the sake of clarity it might help. You have to make a decision as to when one person is identical with something else – is the same person. I was a little baby once; I presume I will be an old person some time, if I am lucky. What makes that little baby the same as the old person? The question 'What is personal identity?' is implied in the question 'What is a person anyway?'. What have you to be to be identical with some obviously clear case of a person? There are clear cases of persons. At least something is clear in this area, and that is that we can identify paradigm cases of persons. The paradigm case of a person is someone who is a rational and sentient agent, an entity which can reflect on its own existence, which can remember what it has done and experienced, which can feel its relation to the world and to other people, and which can plan its future. It is a subject of rational consciousness. I should want to adopt as the key phrase in this respect that a person is a subject of rational consciousness.

Of course there are fuzzy borderlines. There are going to be things about which we are not quite sure whether they are persons or not. There are going to be cases where it is objectively unclear whether they are persons or not. Even if you believe in natural kinds of things there are still going to be borderline cases where it is actually objectively unclear whether something belongs to a natural kind or not. But if a person is a subject of rational consciousness, then at least one can say that nothing that is not a subject of rational consciousness is a person. If there is some entity which has no rational consciousness – which has no consciousness at all – then it is not a person. One might say that it appears to be a necessary condition of having consciousness that you have a brain, so 'no brain, no person'. One can say that a person is dead when the brain stem ceases to function or that if something hasn't got a brain, it is not a person. That seems quite a compelling argument. But the vital point is not the possession of a brain; it is the possession of rational agency. If a person is a rational, sentient agent then nothing which is not a rational sentient agent – and little embryos certainly aren't that – is a person.

That is the first of the views of personal identity – that it consists mainly in being a subject of rational consciousness. You may use as a philosophical tag for that the name of Descartes, although that is not quite fair because it will probably raise all sorts of horrible spectres in people's minds. It is broadly speaking a dualist view nevertheless. To say that a person is a subject of rational consciousness is a form of dualism; it separates mind from body, consciousness from material body and brain.

This immediately leads on to the second theory about personal identity, namely a non-dualist theory or what is often called an identity theory. The identity theory is in fact probably the most fashionable view of personal identity among philosophers at the moment. It consists in saying that a person's experience, and indeed a person's subjectivity, is in the end identical with some set of brain states. There is no radical difference in kind between conscious states and material states. Your conscious states are an aspect of your physical states. On a non-dualist view it is not satisfactory to say that a person is a subject of rational consciousness, as though one took that subject to be disembodied somehow, or as though it were only contingently associated with a particular brain and body. One might rather want to say, not that there is not a subject of rational consciousness, but that that subject is in fact the brain, or that it is in fact that particular physical organism which provides the causal basis of consciousness and all the capacities associated with consciousness. One might say a person is a psycho-physical unity, not a mind plus a body, but just a body which actualizes, or is capable of actualizing, certain distinctively rational characteristics. On the identity thesis, one might say that anything which has a capacity for rational thought is a person and that that capacity must be located in a certain physical constitution of some sort. Then there is the question of what that physical constitution is. We are not talking about a subject, a mind, a soul, a spirit, different from the material elements; but we are saying that there must be a material substance with a natural constitution which is apt for realizing rational capacities.

This is very close to Aristotle's view, and it is a peculiarity of the Catholic tradition, that it blends Aristotle and Plato in a holy mixture which was baptized by Thomas Aquinas. One can see both trains of thought within Aquinas. But on the whole Aquinas wanted to hold *both* that a person is a psycho-physical unity, that the soul is the form of the body, the living organizing principle of a material body, and *also* that the soul is a substantial form rather like God, who is the other sort of substantial form that is capable of existing without the body. In the case of human souls, however, they exist in disembodied form, only in an unnatural and imperfect way. This is a rather complicated doctrine, very different from the simple dualism which is often believed to characterize Christian thought. Catholic theologians tend to argue both that a human person is a psycho-physical unity – not a soul which can exist in its natural state distinct from any body; and also that a person is an entity of a kind to which rational attributes are proper. Thus arises the view that probably the structure of chromosomes in the embryo is the natural constitution of a physical, continuing entity, which is the rational subject of consciousness. That gives the philosophical foundation for the view that a person is a person from the moment of conception.

It is ironic that this view depends so largely upon the identity theory, since Catholic thinkers do allow the possibility of the soul existing substantially, whereas materialist identity-theorists rarely ascribe personhood to early embryos. This fact shows the complex overlapping of different issues in this debate. Materialists usually take a utilitarian view, holding that factual assertions do not determine moral issues; whereas Catholics usually attempt to derive moral principles from the structures of nature, as Divinely created, and to take them as absolutely binding, by God's will. So it is that whereas Catholics and materialists can sound very similar, they come to different ethical conclusions, because they weigh the different sorts of issues at stake differently.

Just to complicate matters further, Thomas Aquinas, one of the most respected late medieval Catholic theologians, believed that the requisite structure for a human soul did not come into being until about six weeks after conception, and that the soul was then created by God. The Catholic Church has not ruled on this matter; but, holding that the soul *may* be created at the moment of conception, it treats experiments on embryos as experiments on human persons. Overall, however, one can see how a dualist view might incline one to place the origin of human personhood at a later stage in embryogenesis than an identity view of personhood.

The third issue that I want to deal with now is the more directly ethical issue of how you take morality to be founded, what you think your moral principles are ultimately based on. I shall grossly oversimplify at this point and sketch two main positions, the utilitarian and the absolutist, though it should be obvious that these are by no means the only options.

What I call the utilitarian view would be the view that in the end ethical decisions are made by taking into account human preferences, and that is the basis of all ethical decisions. There is no other ultimate basis than that. You ask what human beings prefer to do, what their fundamental desires are, and how they can be maximized without causing undue interference with other people's desires. It doesn't have to be as crude as saying you maximize everybody's preferences, or the preferences of the maximum number of people, but some rather weaker view than that. If you are going to have moral rules, what you have to consider are people's desires. The sort of rules you have are going to be made up by you. But you are going to invent them on the basis that these rules will sustain very basic human sentiments which will encourage those things which we and (we think) most rational people would prefer. So, for example, you may think that caring for other people, caring for little children, caring for handicapped people and old people is a good thing. It helps to bind society together, and it would destroy social order if it didn't exist. It would outrage a lot of people if nobody cared for other people. So you come to think that caring for other people is a good, that on the whole it will help our human desires to be fulfilled reasonably. You want to sustain the sentiments of sympathy and compassion which undergird such caring. Your ethical rules will then be those which, in your opinion, will most effectively help to sustain those human sentiments of compassion and sympathy.

You could then argue that torturing little babies to death is probably not going to help to make people more sympathetic and compassionate in general, though torturing animals to death may not matter so much. But you have to make that decision and decide what sorts of activities you think would increase compassion in general. Your moral rules would be designed with that as their end. In general if you are wanting to design your moral rules with the aim of sustaining human sentiments which you take to be of importance in society, that is a broadly utilitarian view. You will not have any principles which will override all other principles absolutely in every situation. It would be a matter of working things out in a rather complicated way, taking a lot of complicated consequences into account, and perhaps changing the rules from time to time.

If you ask about embryos on this sort of approach the question would be 'Would killing embryos' (and I am assuming that experimenting on embryos however produced entails killing them afterwards) 'undermine our human sentiments of compassion and sympathy?'. One would have to look at many consequences and make a probable guess as to whether it would or not. I suppose my own judgement on that would be: no, I do not think that killing embryos would undermine human sentiments, because you could fairly easily persuade people that small embryos don't look like human beings and they are not really like human beings. So, killing them doesn't lead you down the slippery slope to infanticide. If, however, you thought it did lead you down the slippery slope, then you would probably be against it. But the reason you would be against it or for it would be because of the consequences which the rule would have for human sentiments. And those consequences would in turn be judged on the major human preferences which you think ought to be encouraged and sustained.

Unfortunately, people are not going to agree about whether this is the correct basis for making ethical judgements. In the history of philosophy a vast majority of philosophers are committed against the truth or plausibility of this view. If I call the alternative view 'absolutism', I would put it in the words of Immanuel Kant that persons are to be treated as ends in themselves and not solely as means to some other end. There are final limits on human action which must never be overridden and you can never use a person as a means to any end other than their own good. You might take this to be a completely non-utilitarian appeal to justice or human rights. If somebody says, 'Let's see if that actually maximizes human preferences', you would reply as an absolutist, 'I don't consider that a relevant question, in fact that is the beginning of moral decay and corruption'.

The former Professor of Philosophy in Cambridge, Elizabeth Anscombe, held that even to raise the question of whether killing the innocent could be of any consequential benefit was morally corrupt and depraved of itself, because the principle of 'do not kill the innocent' is simply an absolute moral rule. Why it is absolute is perhaps more difficult to explain. I suppose you ground it on the principle that, if something is a person, there are certain things that you must never do in any circumstances and one of the clearest of them is to kill it, if it has not in some way forfeited innocence. So the principle comes out as 'never kill an innocent person, i.e., an innocent human being'. Holding that view you would probably go along with saying that the term 'innocent human being' fits the case of an embryo after conception.

Some things are absolutely forbidden. Philosophers like Alan Gewirth, for example, would hold that view, that there are some things you should never do whatever the consequences because simply it is against the basic notion of human dignity to do it, and they need to be absolutely forbidden. You might believe in addition that God has as a matter of fact absolutely forbidden it, but it is not necessary to the holding of this view to bring God in. You could just hold the view that utilitarianism, even in its broadest sense, cannot account for or justify principles of justice and human rights. If you are going to have such principles at all, you must have them as absolute principles. You are pinning your flag to the mast of human dignity and saying that there are some things you won't ever do – torture or the killing of the innocent are two of the most often mentioned. That is the third issue – utilitarianism and absolutism – on which I think there is an irresolvable dispute.

The fourth issue is about the role of nature and human responsibility. One alternative is to take the rather clear line that in so far as we have knowledge and ability, we are responsible for what we do in the world and we must take responsibility for what we do. We must aim to bring about what is good and eliminate what is bad. What the processes of nature do has got nothing to do with it. Perhaps the best formulated expression of this view is in a paper 'Evolution and Ethics' by T. H. Huxley, in which he argues following Tennyson (I believe) that nature is red in tooth and claw, totally hideous in almost every aspect; that animals live by eating each other, preying on one another, that the natural way of life is the survival of the fittest, the sending of the weak to the wall, the killing of as many people as you can as long as it is to your benefit. Those are the things animals appear to do and that is the natural way. But Huxley said that we should pay no attention to nature and that indeed the only human way to act is to oppose nature and all its works. That is an extreme statement of the view. So, what happens in nature is of no moral relevance whatsoever. You simply have to ask the question: 'Is it good or bad for people?' It is natural for people to get cancer; it is natural for cancer cells to multiply themselves. Does that have any moral relevance? Huxley would say 'none at all'; it is completely morally irrelevant. You simply have to ask whether this is a good thing for people to have; if it is bad then you must oppose it.

But of course clearly there is another position. This is a view which is associated with one particular interpretation of natural law theory. On that interpretation there are purposes of nature and, to put it at its most basic, it is always wrong to frustrate a purpose of nature, that is to say a natural process, at least where that process culminates in a natural and desirable good. That is a view which is held at the moment by the Vatican teaching magisterium. It accounts for the moral prohibition of contraception because that would be frustrating the purpose of nature which is the procreation of children through sexual activity. As applied to embryos, this would mean that once an embryo has begun to develop then that is a natural purpose which will or should or could naturally end in the development of a person and it is wrong then to frustrate that natural purpose. The view at issue is this, 'Is it true that it is always wrong to frustrate a purpose of nature?'. The view that it is labours under enormous difficulties, of which I will mention a few.

One is that many people, sincere and intelligent people, would beg leave to doubt whether there are any purposes in nature at all. Certainly if you were a Darwinian biologist, I think you would say there are no purposes in nature; it is a matter of random mutation and selection by environment and it is simply inappropriate to talk about purposes in this way. If anyone does want to talk about purposes of nature, it is a very difficult position to defend. I suppose that if one believes in God, then one does in some sense have to say that there is a purpose in the existence of the physical world. There is some reason why it is here; it wasn't just a divine oversight. So you do have to talk about the purpose of nature in a sense, but there is quite a large gulf between saying you have to talk about nature as embodying a divine purpose, which might be for the flourishing of sentient rational beings, and the more specific view that the particular methods of sexual reproduction which human beings have are themselves purposively instituted by God. It may be true that they are, but there is no entailment between the belief that God created the universe in order that rational sentient beings should come to be and flourish, and the belief that the particular way in which human beings have sex and produce children is itself divinely intended. You may believe that it is so entailed, but you would need an additional argument to support it.

A very difficult question raised here is the nature of divine providence; so again it is not surprising that there are going to be difficulties about this even among theologians. How does divine providence enter into the structure of the world and the way that things go? Is it the case, for example, that God is (as it were) in direct control of human procreation so that if you just take a chance and have sexual intercourse, then it is up to God whether a child is conceived or not, and if you conceive that is God's will and if you don't that is God's will too? There are people who believe this and they would say this is because divine providence enters into every aspect of human life and particularly of course human procreation – particularly there, because human procreation will lead to souls which are destined for eternal bliss. It is a particularly important point and just as God disposes of human life and decides the moment of death (with which we should not interfere), so perhaps God decides the moment of creation of a new human being. I think this would be a very difficult view for which to argue, considering for a start the enormous number of spontaneous abortions unnoticed by the mothers in question and considering (as I am informed by medical colleagues) that most fertilized ova will not implant. It seems a very odd way for divine providence to be involved.

The deeper question, however, is this: supposing human responsibility could determine the moment of conception, then would it always have to be the case that we should not do so because we had to leave it to God? I would not myself say this about any other area of human activity. When I cross the road I don't leave it to God whether I get knocked over or not, I have a look and see what is coming and exercise a bit of responsibility. I would have thought that the same thing would be true of procreation. (It should be said that the present Pope, who has very strong views on these subjects, nevertheless accepts in principle that there could be methods of controlling the procreation of children as long as those methods did not involve frustrating natural processes. The interesting point is that you could *control* a natural process but not frustrate it. If that is a possibility, then human responsibility at least has a look-in. I would be tempted to suggest that, once you have given it a look-in, you have to let it have quite a sphere of activity and not say 'thus far and no further', or 'now I am going to leave it to chance and let nature take its course'. Forsaking neutrality in this instance, I think that 'letting nature take its course' is deeply immoral, reprehensible and irrational.)

I have looked at four very different philosophical issues, all of which are essentially contestable. My own views have probably come over to some extent, but I will make them much clearer in ending. We are faced with what William James called 'a vital living and forced option', that is to say we have to decide whether to experiment on embryos or not. We don't have any possibility of not making a decision. It is one which is very important to make, so we can't sit on the fence. All we can do is attend to the arguments, assess the probable weight (as it seems to us) of what they are, and then commit ourselves to acting even in uncertainty. I regard this as perhaps a most important *philosophical* conclusion of the whole debate, that you often have to commit yourself in objective uncertainty with an absolute commitment in areas where the probabilities are very differently weighed by different people. That has very great implications for many human beliefs.

I am an Anglican theologian and so I stand within an Anglican tradition. I don't mean to malign either atheists or Roman Catholics or anybody else, but I do have to say I disagree with quite a lot of other people. I am committed to believing that God created the universe and did so for a purpose. However, I am also committed to a Darwinian view of evolution on general grounds of intellectual honesty, and to the view that this is compatible with God having a purpose for the world, namely that God set it up so that things would develop through the processes of random mutation by which they have developed. That means I am not going to be disposed to say that nature should be left as it is. Rather I would say that nature, even though created by God, is in many ways imperfect, and that suffering is always to be opposed in all its forms and any legitimate means to help to overcome it must be taken. Experiments on embryos of course offer a very great possible benefit to eliminating grievous hereditary disorders such as spina bifida, and I think that anything morally legitimate must be done to help to overcome such disorders.

The question then is of course: is it morally legitimate to experiment on embryos which have been created *in vitro*, not by processes of human procreation? These are not in any straightforward sense embryos which will *naturally*, by a natural process of nature, become human persons. They will certainly not. Since they have been created on a glass dish in a laboratory they will not naturally become human persons unless you do a lot more complicated things with them to which there might be other moral objections. One cannot even properly speak of them, therefore, as 'potential persons', in the obvious sense. Now I accept the argument that persons are kinds of entities to which it is proper to have rational capacities. I am not a verificationist. I do think that the question 'When is something a person?' is a real and proper question, and I would suggest that it is neither a necessary nor a sufficient condition for being a person that one has forty-six chromosomes. There could be something with forty-six or forty-seven chromosomes which was not a person and there could be something which was a person which did not have that number of chromosomes. Personal identity is in fact a thing which contains many different strands and one strand, which is decisive for me, is that a necessary condition of being a person is the possession of rational consciousness, or at least the possession of the subjecthood of rational consciousness.

Finally, I am not an absolutist in ethics, and incline to think that all moral principles should be assessed in terms of their contribution to specific human or divine goals – goals wider than that of simply happiness.

Given these attitudes to the four main questions I have addressed briefly in this chapter, the view to which I find myself drawn is that embryos at a developmental stage prior to the formation of a brain, a necessary condition of conscious life, are not human persons. It is thus morally permissible to conduct experiments which promise a great and otherwise unobtainable good for persons, since there is no possibility of causing pain or distress to the organism. Further, I would regard this as part of the proper exercise of human responsibility for eliminating suffering and gross malfunction from the natural world as far as possible.

What I have sought to bring out is the way in which ethical decisions of this nature are bound up with a complex of questions about the nature of human knowledge, of human life, of morality and of divine providence. Each of these questions is of great complexity, and a given person may make any combination of answers to them, producing a huge variety of permutations, which will govern the process of moral decision-making in a particular case. I have described each quesion as being essentially contestable. That does not mean that there is no correct answer to them. It means that there is no way of establishing the truth of any such answer, to the satisfaction of all competent disputants. In such a situation, what ethical discussion can and should do is to try to ensure that all disputants are fully informed participants in a rational discussion. In this way, they can clarify the consequences of their own position, become aware of the arguments for differing positions, and accept a common commitment to achieve a coherent and defensible overall ethical view. What ethics can do is to make clear what the issues are, and what justifying reasons have been offered in support of them. Philosophical ethics will never bring agreement. But it may bring increased understanding, increased concern for rationality, and increased clarity and self-knowledge. And that is surely a much better base from which to make moral decisions.

Chapter eight

Experimentation: some legal aspects

Douglas J. Cusine

The subject of research on human embryos is probably one of the aspects of The Warnock Committee's deliberations which has attracted greatest publicity.[1] The other one is of course surrogacy. We have now got to the stage where much else in The Warnock Report has by and large been forgotten by a substantial part of the public. I think the crucial issue which was facing The Warnock Committee and faces us still today is whether research on human embryos should be allowed and, if so, in what circumstances and subject to what control. In the course of this chapter I consider this subject under several headings.

First, what protection, if any, should one afford to the human embryo, and why? At what point should the protection begin? For how long should research be carried out, if at all? What kinds of research? By whom should the research be monitored and how, if at all, should it be controlled? Now, one of the interesting features of The Warnock Report is that it did not in fact define the term 'research'. The report said that it covers two broad categories, the 'pure' research which was aimed at increasing and developing our knowledge of human embryos, and the 'applied' research which has direct relevance for the patients. But it seems that a great deal of research is merely observation. To put it somewhat crudely, scientists may peer down a microscope and observe what happens and, as a result of these observations, come up with a theory which they test by further experimentation. So, if one is talking about banning research on human embryos, one must be clear exactly what is meant by 'research'. Very few people have attempted to find out exactly what is meant by 'research' when they have said that research on human embryos should be banned.

I want to outline some of the arguments against research and some of the arguments for research. Then I will be bold enough to give my own view on where we should be going from here. Some people are fundamentally opposed to 'research on human embryos', however that phrase is defined, because for them the embryo is either a human being, or it is a potential human being, entitled to the protection which we afford to other human beings. These people say that research can take place on human beings only with those human beings' informed consent and, because an embryo is incapable of giving that consent, then the research cannot be carried out. Research, they would go on to say, deprives the embryo of its life or its potential life.

Again, other people are genuinely concerned about research because they feel that it is tampering with human life. They would express fears about mad doctors, mad scientists, even mad governments, producing creatures which exemplify their theories on breeding and eugenics. Many who are opposed to research would undoubtedly accept that a great deal of valuable information can be lost by not doing the research. Nevertheless, they feel that their moral stance requires them to override these advantages in favour of prohibiting research. Some of the objections are to be found in the expression of dissent by three of the members of The Warnock Committee. The view of the majority of The Warnock Committee was, however, that research should be carried out until the fourteenth day after fertilization and thereafter the embryo would be entitled to the same protection as would be afforded to any other fetus. The dissenters' view was that the embryo has a special status because of its potential and accordingly it should be given protection at all stages.

The arguments in favour of research are numerous. The more important ones are that it would allow us to develop our knowledge of the process of fertilization, of contraception, and of congenital defects and other inheritable diseases. The commonly expressed view is that human embryos are entitled to more respect than animal subjects, but that such respect does not involve an absolute protection. The Warnock Committee was convinced of substantial benefits to be had from the research. That, in its view, outweighed the arguments against conducting research on embryos. (In this connection I note, in passing, Professor Gordon Dunstan's article on 'The moral status of the human embryo: a tradition recalled'.[2] He traces the various ethical attitudes to the question of protection being afforded to embryos and indicates that the notion of protection being afforded from fertilization can be traced to the mid-nineteenth century and no earlier.)

I now look in more detail at the 'absolutist' view as against the view which requires some but not absolute protection. Here it is useful to make a number of clarifications.

When people say that the embryo is 'human' or 'potentially

human', they frequently assert that this 'human being' or 'potential human being' exists from 'the moment of fertilization'. Others talk about 'the moment of conception'. There is a great deal of confusion about these two terms. Many people, particularly in the Parliamentary debates on The Warnock Report, got into total confusion by using them interchangeably. We should be clear that both of these terms – fertilization and conception – refer to processes, not to events. Fertilization and conception cannot be pinpointed as taking place at a particular point in time. The fertilization process creates a fertilized egg which then has to make its way into the uterine cavity, where it becomes implanted into the wall of the uterus and then develops into a fetus. That process takes some considerable time. The reason why The Warnock Committee suggested fourteen days as the limit which they would impose upon research was that, prior to day fourteen, one cannot be clear that what appears to be an embryo will turn out to be one embryo or perhaps even twins. At that stage it is possible also that what looks like an embryo is in fact something approximating to a cancerous growth which may have to be removed surgically at some later stage. So it is important, if one is talking about giving protection, that one is clear on why protection is being given and that one does not use terms like 'fertilization' and 'conception' in a confusing manner.

I have been asked to talk about the legal aspects of these matters. In fact, there is not a lot of law in this area at the moment. We are at the stage of inventing what it ought to be. Some people make reference to existing law in connection with their arguments for protection. But I must confess to some difficulty in trying to extrapolate from the areas of law with which I am familiar to any kind of protection for the human embryo as it exists. Where, broadly speaking, the law does give protection is to a fetus which is part of the mother. It is protected in that sense by the abortion legislation so that abortion can take place only in circumstances allowed under the Abortion Act. Another area in which the law recognizes the existence of a fetus is where, in certain circumstances, it gives damages in respect of antenatal injuries. But in both of these cases it is important to realize that there is a fetus and a pregnant woman and, as far as the damages for antenatal injuries are concerned, these will arise only if the child is born alive. That said, in my view there is nothing at present in the common law of England, certainly nothing in the common law of Scotland, and nothing in statute law, which would allow us to suggest that protection is given to the embryo at the stage prior to implantation.

If this is the case, then we have the somewhat peculiar situation that the embryo *in vitro*, in the laboratory, is not protected at all by the law. And if it is not a human being, then I would suggest that it is, as far as the law is concerned at the moment, no more than an item of property. That notion may horrify people, but it seems that, as the law stands at the moment, if it is not a human being then it can only be an item of property. If that is so, then there is nothing to prevent experimentation on the human embryo. There is nothing to prevent one using it as one would any other item of property. Let me give what I regard as a fairly scary example. If the embryo is not afforded protection, then it is possible to dispose of the embryo by will, e.g., to an infertile daughter. So a couple who have an embryo could have it frozen and stored; the embryo could then be subsequently implanted into the couple's daughter. The lucky embryo would then end up with two mothers, one genetic father and one social father. It would then have two sets of parents. That is a highly unlikely scenario but, as the law stands at the moment, it is theoretically possible.

What I have been suggesting for a long time is that we need some kind of legislative clarification. It is highly irresponsible for a government to allow people involved in human reproduction to operate in legal darkness. We are not talking about a grey area, but about legal darkness. Government ought to come out one way or another on this issue. When the then Secretary of State for Social Services announced in Parliament the setting up of The Warnock Committee, he almost congratulated himself for having the foresight to do this. Many people, including some politicians, do not actually pay any attention to what is going on in the field of medicine. Professor Robert Edwards has been working on *in vitro* fertilization since 1965 at least. In a very valuable article published as long ago as 1974, Edwards reviewed many of the issues in this connection.[3] It should have been clear to the Government that if Edwards and Steptoe were working on *in vitro* fertilization then, they were almost inevitably going to produce embryos in due course.

Where should we go from here? There are, broadly speaking, two possibilities. First one can provide legislation which prohibits *in vitro* fertilization. That, it seems, would have been the effect of the Powell Bill had it been passed. The Powell Bill would have allowed obstetricians to have in their possession embryos solely for the purposes of reimplanting those embryos into women so that they could carry a child. The problem is that, if one is going to permit *in vitro* fertilization then one must accept a possibility that the embryo or some of the embryos which are produced are going to be defective. After they are examined under the microscope it may be judged dangerous to reimplant a certain embryo either because it would not implant, or because it would create a spontaneous abortion, or because a defective child might result. They would be faced with the problem of what to do with that embryo. If the embryo is sacrosanct from fertilization onwards, then it seems that one cannot carry out *in vitro* fertilization because one might have a defective embryo. The second possibility of course is to permit *in vitro* fertilization and ask the scientist to ignore the fact that he or she may have a defective embryo in the laboratory. The scientist would be required, without examining the embryos at all, to reimplant them all. In my view, for that stance to be adopted by scientists would be highly irresponsible.

I personally favour the conduct of research on human embryos. I do not however want to give the scientists *carte blanche* in this field; I do not think they want it. But legislation in this particular area has to tread a delicate path in attempts to reconcile two perhaps conflicting points of view. The conflict is as follows. On the part of any person conducting research as a part of their job, there is an obligation to increase and advance human understanding. This principle may however conflict with another principle, namely that research ought to be conducted within the existing moral framework of the country in which the research is done. But because this apparent conflict exists is no excuse for delaying further activity in this field. If we wait until all the benefits or, if you like, all the disadvantages of research in this area are uncovered, then we will wait indefinitely. The worst thing is to sit on the fence, waiting to see what happens, because what in fact happens is that a particular occurrence achieves notoriety in the newspapers causing the government to produce hasty legislation.

First of all, we need a system which will allow the research to continue subject to the protection which people would regard as appropriate, the protection being that the research should be carried out in keeping with the feelings of the community. To this end, I would strongly suggest that we need primary legislation which introduces, as The Warnock Committee suggested, a licensing system. The people who carry out this research, the institutions in which the research is carried out, and the type of research carried out, must be licensed. But it is not enough to *create* a licensing system. The licensing system must be *seen* to operate. People must go round, inspect these premises, and ensure that unauthorized activities do not take place. It is not enough to say that people who do unauthorized research will not get their results published; the damage is then already done.

There is of course a difficult choice, whether one has the licensing system enshrined in legislation, detailing all the requirements for obtaining a licence, or whether one has some kind of licensing authority, as The Warnock Committee recommended. Either is possible. But the problem with encapsulating all the minutiae in legislation is that, given the pressure of parliamentary time, it is extremely difficult to get legislation changed once it is there. The only legislation which changes rapidly is legislation dealing with taxation and company law. Other areas of legislation are very often simply left because there is not enough parliamentary interest in the particular topic. In that connection, embryo research would not exactly seem to be, a vote-catching subject; it may be the very opposite in some areas. What we require – and this is my own view – is a licensing authority such as The Warnock Committee recommended.

Second, the Committee, perhaps skilfully, avoided saying too precisely who should be on this licensing authority. One important omission from their suggestions was that of a lawyer. It would be essential to have a lawyer on a licensing authority such as this, for it has to operate within the legal constraints laid down by Parliament. The lawyer must give his/her views on consent and on what are the likely legal outcomes of particular types of activity. Obviously the authority must have representatives from the medical profession and from the variety of people who may have an interest from a medical standpoint in this type of research. Beyond that, it is not easy to say. Obviously there are ethical questions to be considered. But a difficulty in this respect is that one cannot identify any one ethical school of thought to which everyone in this country would subscribe. That is why this research cannot be permitted or banned along religious lines. Certainly some ethical input is needed – perhaps from a moral or social theologian or a combination of these two. One last group of people who almost certainly ought to be represented is the general public. How exactly they should be represented on the licensing authority is hard to say; but it is absolutely essential that the views of the man or woman in the street, in so far as it is possible to communicate that view, ought to be available to the licensing authority. There is a great danger that if the licensing is left to the professionals, they will regulate it in the way that they think professional people at large would like this licensing system to operate. The matters that give cause for concern are often those which concern the man or woman in the street.

Third, for how long in the life of the embryo should research be carried out? The Warnock Committee came down in favour of a fourteen-day period for the reason mentioned above. It has been suggested by the Royal College of Obstetricians and Gynaecologists that day seventeen would be an appropriate day because that is the beginning of the formation of the embryonic disc. At one stage Professor Edwards suggested that, if the end of life is the death of the brain stem, then the beginning of the protection ought to be when the brain stem begins. That, I understand, is about day thirty. But it seems fair to say that the consensus is day fourteen. That is the view which various commissions around the world, as in Australia and in Canada, have favoured. That is the figure which the Government, if and when it acts, will probably favour.

One of the problems which arises is whether that fourteen-day period should be a fixed period or should be subject to alteration. Theoretically, if it is part of an Act of Parliament it is capable of being altered, but I have already made clear my views on that. The figure could be alterable on a recommendation of the licensing authority. That does not necessarily mean that we are on a slippery slope. Even if it does, it is not impossible to erect barriers on the slippery slope provided that the licensing system is operated in the way suggested above.

In conclusion, whatever else is required, we do not want to continue for the next five years in the way that we have continued in the last five. In the last five years we have witnessed The Warnock Committee begin and end its work. We have witnessed singularly uninformed discussion in the House of Lords, in the House of Commons, and in the Press. We have witnessed hasty legislation on surrogacy, and an attempt to amend that legislation because it was seen as hasty – an attempt which has not yet succeeded. In view of the various discussion papers the Government has produced, and given the speed at which government processes of consultation operate, it would not be surprising to find that the Government was not in a position to introduce legislation for quite some time.

Many people would not accept my willingness to permit research on human embryos. But surely most people would be of the opinion that we need legislative clarity. Legislative clarity can only do good for everyone involved. If it prohibited research then obviously embryologists, obstetricians, and others would be disappointed, but at least they would know where they stood. If research was to be permitted, then obviously people who are against such research would be disappointed, but at least again they would know where they stood. The last thing we want is darkness, legislatively speaking, for the next five years.

Notes

1 Department of Health and Social Security, *Report of the Committee of Inquiry into Human Fertilisation and Embryology* (London: HMSO, 1984).

2 G. R. Dunstan, 'The moral status of the human embryo: a tradition recalled', *Journal of Medical Ethics* 10 (1984).

3 R. G. Edwards, 'Fertilisation of human eggs in vitro: morals, ethics and the law', *The Quarterly Review of Biology* 49.1 (1974) 3–26.

Chapter nine

The challenge for Parliament: a critique of the White Paper on *Human Fertilisation and Embryology*

Margaret Brazier

Nearly ten years after the birth of Louise Brown and three and a half years after the publication of The Warnock Report,[1] the Government in November 1987 finally presented to Parliament its proposals for the regulation of reproductive medicine and embryology in the United Kingdom. But actual legislation to lighten the legal darkness in which doctors and scientists now operate may have to wait a further year. The White Paper on *Human Fertilisation and Embryology: a Framework for Legislation*[2] makes several detailed proposals. A Statutory Licensing Authority is to be established to license those providing infertility services and additionally (*inter alia*) to license and control storage of human embryos and gametes, to advise on medical and scientific developments, and to formulate a Code of Practice on infertility treatment and embryology. The status of children born as a result of egg or embryo donation is to be clarified.[3] Provision is made for counselling of embryo and gamete donors, and for limited access to information about their genetic parents for the children of such donors. Yet on the central and fundamental question of whether or not to permit the continuation of embryo experimentation in the United Kingdom Government has formulated no definitive proposal.

Legislation prepared as a result of the White Paper will offer Parliament alternative draft clauses on the following lines:

[A] It will be a criminal offence to carry out any procedures on a human embryo other than those aimed at preparing the embryo for transfer to the uterus of a woman: or those carried out to ascertain the suitability of that embryo for the intended transfer.

[B] Except as a part of a project specifically licensed by the Statutory Licensing Authority, it will be a criminal offence to carry out any procedures on a human embryo other than those aimed at preparing the embryo for transfer to the uterus of a woman: or those carried out to ascertain the suitability of that embryo for the intended transfer.

The draft legislation will make it clear that Option A (prohibiting research) will not prohibit the storage of embryos nor the destruction of any defective embryo not suitable for implantation. Option B, which permits research under licence from the Statutory Licensing Authority, will offer only limited freedom to that body to control research. No licence may be granted for the use of embryos beyond fourteen days, or the development of the primitive streak, whichever is the earlier. Certain procedures including genetic manipulation of the embryo and the creation of hybrids are to be absolutely prohibited.

The White Paper justifies the absence of a positive proposal from the Government on embryo experimentation on the grounds that it is for Parliament to take its own view on the fundamental principles involved in the decision whether to permit or prohibit research using human embryos. Thus by analogy with abortion and capital punishment, embryo experimentation as an issue touching on the sanctity of life is left to the conscience of each individual Member of Parliament. But the provision of alternative draft clauses on research and the consequent abrogation of direct government responsibility for the eventual decision is also highly convenient for the Government. It ensures that the odium which a decision to allow research would create among many fundamentalist Christians and Jews will not attach to the Government. The difficulty for the Cabinet of themselves arriving at a collective decision is sidestepped. The Government offends neither those several Tory backbenchers who supported Enoch Powell's Unborn Children (Protection) Bill, nor those of their own supporters who equally forcefully opposed that Bill.

Such a compromise begs a number of questions.

1 Do the alternative draft proposals offer Parliament rational options on which to determine fundamental principles relating to the status of the embryo?
2 When a Bill is finally presented, can Parliament collectively debate embryo experimentation so as to achieve a reasoned conclusion on whether to permit or prohibit research? Or is any debate likely to degenerate into mutual abuse and expressions of sentiment rather than reason?
3 Are the options put to Parliament in the White Paper workable and enforceable?

Rational options?

The alternative draft clauses (Options A and B) outlined in the White Paper offer Parliament something considerably less than freedom to determine fundamental principles relating to the legal and moral status of the human embryo. Option A does not affirm the full humanity of the embryo created *in vitro*. It protects the embryo only from interference via intrusive research procedures, and not from destruction. Option B is equally limited. The Statutory Licensing Authority is to be empowered only to license projects to research on embryos up to fourteen days of development and statutory restrictions are to be imposed on the types of research to be permitted. There is no Option C to offer the prospect of research to any later date, as Professors Edwards[4] and Ward[5] would like. Nor, it seems, can the fourteen-day limit, if enacted, be extended other than by Parliament itself. Options A and B are in themselves compromise proposals; the principles on which each option itself is based and the exclusion of any further options must now be examined.

Option A: prohibiting research

The basic intent of Option A is to attempt to prohibit embryo experimentation while limiting any consequent damage to the IVF programme. Necessarily then, procedures involving observation of the embryo in the Petri dish and aimed at preparing the embryo for transfer to the mother will not be prohibited. Nor will the legislation prohibit the storage of embryos, or impinge on the practice of inducing super-ovulation to create 'spare' embryos, not all of which will be implanted in the mother. Surplus embryos will be 'allowed to perish' either if unsuitable for implantation, or if the donors withhold their consent to storage of 'their' embryos, or, if unused before then, at the expirty of the five-year storage period proposed by the White Paper.[6]

Option A thus sanctions the creation of embryos 'doomed to die'. That accords the embryo *in vitro* less than fully human status, so can Option A itself be ethically acceptable to people who maintain that from the fusion of egg and sperm a genetically unique person is created who is as entitled to the law's protection as any born child or adult human being? I think that this can be achieved only at the cost of compromising to some extent any absolutist view of the humanity of the embryo from the conclusion of the fertilization process. That compromise cannot be based on a preference for destruction over research *per se*. 'Killing' an embryo by washing it down the drain cannot in itself be morally preferable to researching on the embryo (at a time when it is certain that the embryo can feel no pain) before washing it down the drain. So other grounds for compromise must be sought.

There are perhaps at least three possible grounds. First, the creation of embryos 'doomed to die' could be prevented only by prohibiting the practice of super-ovulation of patients scheduled for IVF treatment and the consequent creation of 'spare' embryos. This would effectively stultify and maybe destroy the IVF programme itself. If doctors could harvest only one egg at a time, chances of establishing a successful pregnancy by implanting three or four embryos would be lost. Freezing embryos would necessarily have to be prohibited. This would mean women would have to submit to several interventions to secure eggs, at extra expense and stress to them. The arguments for not prohibiting the creation of spare embryos sounds forceful. But once it is conceded that damaging the prospects of successful IVF treatment justifies the inevitable destruction of *some* embryos, the case against research is significantly weakened. Is the IVF programme a greater moral imperative than the potential to reduce or eliminate genetic defects?

The two other grounds for the compromise in Option A are the inherent instability of all early embryos, and the contention that deliberate interference with embryos is of a different moral order to 'allowing embryos to perish'. *In vivo*, many fertilized eggs do not implant in the uterus,[7] others implant briefly but are lost before the woman knows herself pregnant, in what may seem to be just a slightly late or heavy period. So is losing a few embryos *in vitro* morally very different? Again the argument confounds itself. If losing a few human lives is no big deal, why cannot they be lost usefully via research? Only if the contention can be upheld that deliberate interference is of a different order to incidental destruction, can Option A in its present form be justified.[8] And that depends on accepting that the crucial issue is the *intent* of those dealing with the embryo. It would be permissible to create a human being, hoping and intending that it fulfil its potential as an embryo growing within a woman to become a child, albeit knowing that that intent might not be attained. It is not permissible to interfere with that embryo for purposes of no benefit for it. That is a derogation from the humanity of the embryo.

While the latter argument is the most convincing, it still fails, I think, to make the case for the compromise entailed in Option A. Full respect for embryos demands that the deliberate creation of 'spare' embryos be stopped.[9] Not even Enoch Powell's Bill demanded that drastic measure. But it is an inevitable consequence of according to the embryo the full moral and legal status of a human person. The failure by some of the opponents of embryo experimentation to address this issue[10] is understandable.

The case against research alone has a much more dramatic profile. Instinctive revulsion for what may be seen as the imminent prospect of a 'Brave New World' can be invoked to gain mass support for not experimenting on 'babies'. IVF is a much more tricky target. IVF creates sweet little babies at the end of the day, albeit for only a small percentage of hopeful parents. But the issue of the status of the embryo *in vitro* is one and the same. An embryo whose legal and moral status demands protection from research equally merits protection from destruction.

Option B: permitting research

Option B, which if enacted would permit limited research on human embryos specifically licensed by the Statutory Licensing Authority, is once again a carefully designed compromise proposal intended maybe to maximize Parliamentary support for permitting research. The time limit of fourteen days from placing the egg and sperm together for fertilization recommended by Warnock is adopted. Practices which raise the spectre of mad scientists tampering with the human race are specifically banned. Thus the Government seeks to avoid any claim that research, if permitted at all, takes us onto the 'slippery slope' towards science fiction nightmares.

Four categories of potential research projects will be banned by the draft Bill. The first two prohibited categories seek to allay fears of the creation of a master race and/or sub-categories of specially designed humans. Thus genetic manipulation of the embryo to create a being with 'certain pre-determined characteristics through modification of the early embryo's genetic structure', and research into the production of clones are to be outlawed. The remaining prohibited categories deal with trans-species research. The Bill will prohibit transfer to a human uterus, or vice versa, of any hybrid embryo combining human and non-human gametes. Trans-species fertilization *in vitro* will itself be forbidden except for the purpose of assessing sub-fertility. The 'hamster test' to investigate the quality of human sperm will thus remain lawful. but anyone permitting development of a trans-species fertilized egg beyond the two-cell stage will commit a criminal offence.

The choice of prohibited categories of research occasions little comment. The procedures selected to ban unacceptable research are of more interest. The proposed legislation will be flexible. Provision is made both for Parliament by affirmative regulation to make exceptions to the prohibited categories if new developments make such a measure appropriate, and also to extend the categories of prohibited research by regulation. This is in marked contrast to the decision to opt for an absolute time limit of fourteen days from fertilization after which further research becomes a criminal offence.

In the White Paper at least no provision is made for extension of that limit other than by repeal of the legislation and its replacement by a new governing statute.[11]

The inflexibility of the fourteen-day time-limit on research enforceable by criminal penalties raises the question of why the options before Parliament were limited to two. Why is there no Option C? This could have embodied either a more flexible fourteen-day limit open to extension by regulation, or a fixed but much longer limit expiring 28–40 days after fertilization. The selection of a fourteen-day limit by Warnock depended on their choice as a reference point of the formation of the primitive streak marking the beginning of the individual development of the embryo. This represents the latest stage at which identical twins can develop and by that time it is possible to tell whether the cells will continue to develop as an embryo or may constitute an abnormality such as hydatidiform mole. The key to a fourteen-day limit rests on individuality. No research should take place once the embryo has developed the markers that indicate that it could develop as a single individual.

But offering Parliament only a fourteen-day option ignores much of the current literature on the status of the embryo. Why is the potential to be a single individual embryo so crucial to its status? After all, the majority of fertilized eggs will achieve this; only a small minority become identical twins or abnormal growths. Interesting support is given by ethicists,[12] including distinguished theologians,[13] to the view that it is 'brain life' which marks the beginning of humanity, as it is accepted 'brain death' marks its end. What distinguishes the human from other species is the capacity to reason. Only when the organs vital to that capacity begin to develop does a human embryo acquire a status deserving of legal protection.[14] The exclusion of an option representing this perception of the status of the embryo restricts the debate on fundamental principles postulated in the White Paper.

Does this matter, though? After all, the function of Parliament is not to operate as a rational forum for ethical dispute. What the Government has done is not to entrust to Parliament a decision on the fundamental principles relating to the status of the human embryo, but to ask them to select between two acceptable compromises.[15] They have sought to ensure that neither option is too unpalatable. Option A prohibiting research nevertheless preserves the IVF programme. Option B permitting research is restricted to a period when the embryo if pictured in the popular Press bears no resemblance to a baby.

A reasoned debate?

What are the prospects that when Parliament considers the options before them on research they will in reality seek to examine and dispute fundamental principles relating to research on human embryos? Two factors diminish the prospects for such a debate. First, the White Paper was scheduled for debate at the same time as David Alton's Private Member's Bill to ban abortion from 18 weeks of pregnancy.[16] Second, the emotions generated by embryo research tend to polarize discussion into one group who view medical research on embryos as a *quasi-Nazi* abomination, opposed by others who regard any opposition to research as rooted in superstition and Luddite tendencies. When even such an intellectual as Enoch Powell introduced his Bill to prohibit research as grounded on his 'invincible repugnance', what hope is there for his fellows?

Predicting how Honourable Members will react to the options on research presented to them is a task for the political analyst or the clairvoyant. But on what criteria should Parliament debate these issues? Three primary issues must be addressed. The benefits claimed for embryo research must be assessed, the legal and moral status of the early embryo must be established, and the relevance of public feelings about research must be explored. The feasibility of the objects of research is a matter beyond the scope of this chapter. Thus the pros and cons of research will be examined only to the extent to which those arguments relate to the disputed status of the embryo and their impact on popular opinion about the ethics of research.

At present the embryo created *in vitro* lacks any legal status in England. The legislation, dating from 1861, protecting embryos *in vivo* from abortion requires the procurement of a miscarriage.[17] An embryo never carried within a woman thus falls beyond the reach of the criminal law designed to protect the unborn. The moral status of that embryo, however, should not differ simply because of the mode of its creation. If a thirteen-day embryo within its mother is entitled to the law's protection, then the thirteen-day embryo in the laboratory deserves similar legal status.[18]

Either Option A or Option B meets to some extent the demand for recognition of the status of the embryo *in vitro*. The embryo is afforded legal protection from unauthorized interference. It would cease to be in legal terms simply an item of property whose ownership is unclear. But how far should the analogy between the embryo *in vivo* or *in vitro* be pursued? Does it follow that opponents of research must necessarily oppose all abortions?

The central issue in answering this question is what legal consequences flow from the disputed moral status of the embryo.[19]

The difficulty is that the dispute is itself incapable of any conclusive resolution. Perception of the status of the embryo derives in many cases from the presence or absence of religious belief. Most, but not all, proponents of the belief that the embryo is from fertilization a genetically unique individual as fully human as you or I, rest that belief, at least in part, on the embryo's potential possession of an immortal, immaterial soul. Professor Ward, who shares that belief in ensoulment, argues forcefully that the very early embryo is unlikely to be ensouled until the beginnings of brain development.[20] Many, but again by no means all, proponents of allowing research on embryos deny or doubt the existence of the soul.

Thus the argument on abortion becomes for opponents: 'How can the law permit the wanton destruction of human life?' And supporters of liberal abortion laws respond: 'By what right do you seek to impose your personal unprovable claims about God and the soul on others?' The dispute reaches stalemate and the debate on embryo research looks set to reach the same result. Legislators must be prepared to look beyond their individual moral and religious beliefs. The humanity of the embryo is unproven and unprovable. But that acts both ways. Just as I cannot prove that humanity was divinely created and that each and every one of us possesses an immortal soul, so it cannot be proved that it is *not* so. Admitting the possibility of the soul, the moment of ensoulment cannot be proved. Nothing more or less can be concluded about the full humanity of the embryo save to say that the cases for and against are, to borrow a Scottish term, not proven.

What consequences follow from a not proven verdict? Herein lies the crucial distinction between abortion and research. When a woman is pregnant with a child in circumstances where the pregnancy threatens her health or those of her existing children, her humanity and that of her born children are beyond doubt. She enjoys full human rights, including the right to autonomy. If she believes, as I do, that from fertilization any embryo within her shares her status she cannot ethically abort that embryo save for very grave cause. A woman who does not share such a belief cannot be compelled to act on a proposition which is unprovable, however sincerely held by others. The decision whether to permit women to terminate a pregnancy must always attain a balance between her undeniable rights as a human person, and the legitimate claims of the embryo.[21] Total prohibition of abortion is thus unthinkable in a democratic liberal society where there is such a divergence of belief in the nature of humanity.

Embryo research involves no such conflict of rights. The embryo is an entity which may be human. It is arguably as entitled to protection as any child or adult. Just as its unproven status requires that when its rights conflict with its mother's, hers must have priority, so where no other person's rights are in issue the embryo's rights demand protection.[22] What of society's rights? It could be argued that if a 'maybe human' may be sacrificed to uphold the rights of an individual female, then there is a good case for sacrificing such an entity in the 'public good'. Improving infertility treatment and eliminating genetic defects may be advanced as 'public goods'. Parliament must address this carefully. It cannot be denied that the law and Christian society has in the past fairly cavalierly sacrificed indubitably human persons in the 'public good'.

The not proven status of the embryo has this result: the onus of establishing that the law should permit interference with and destruction of the embryo lies on those who put the case *for* research. They must convince Parliament that the benefits which will flow from research (within the fourteen-day period)[23] justify abrogation of the embryo's rights. Too often it has seemed that the debate is weighted the other way, requiring opponents of research to justify not interfering with embryos if there is *any* arguably good outcome for the research. The burden of proof rests rather on the proponents of experimentation.

Parliament, however, is not a committee of inquiry nor a jury weighing and sifting evidence. The 'evidence' before them will be supplemented by individual Members' feelings on the issue and pressure from constituents. Letters will pour in urging Honourable Members to have nothing to do with such barbaric practices. Other letters pressing for research to be permitted will recount anguished tales of the effect on families of genetic disease and the trauma of infertility. Much has been written condemning emotionalism in decision-making on such issues as embryo research. Baroness Warnock in particular has been criticized for arguing that people's instinctive feelings about the developing embryo should be taken into account in framing legislation.[24]

There is simply no way in which Parliament can or should discount popular feelings. That is not to say they should slavishly follow popular opinion. Parliament must evaluate that opinion. Opponents of research (and abortion) are often accused of playing on our emotions. They are not alone in doing so; proponents of research skilfully and quite properly exploit the distress and trauma of infertility. They present the case for advancing and developing IVF, embryo donation and research as a women's rights issue in an attempt to maximize female support for embryo research.

Members of Parliament enacting legislation must seek to examine the basis of the emotions played upon by both proponents and opponents of experimentation. Embryo research up to a limit of fourteen days or even forty days is not the same as experimenting on babies. Such procedures cannot cause pain or distress either to the embryo or to other persons emotionally bonded to the embryo. Seeking to maximize support for banning research by emotively calling the embryo an unborn child is not helpful. The case against research rests on the moral perception of the undeveloped embryo as nonetheless human and the belief that interference with humans is wrong and unacceptable. Repugnance to thus tampering with humanity itself generates powerful emotions. It is those emotions which Parliament must assess, not false analogies with hurting babies.

The appeal to feelings made by proponents of research must also be carefully scrutinized. Is prohibiting research an affront to women and an infringement of the 'right to reproduce'? Such a ban will undoubtedly cause real distress to infertile women whose chances of a baby via improved IVF and related procedures are damaged. The impact on women in society generally is less clear. Feminist support for modern reproductive medicine is far from uniform. Disquiet is expressed on several issues. Embryo experimentation demands a constant supply of eggs. Can a woman who is already a patient dependent on her gynaecologist either for fertility treatment or for sterilization or hysterectomy make an untrammelled choice of whether to accede to his request to donate eggs? Is it ethical to subject a woman scheduled for hysterectomy to a procedure unrelated to that surgery to produce enough eggs to be worth harvesting?[25] The concept of a 'right to reproduce' is itself doubted as either existing or desirable. The right to found a family[26] does not carry with it a correlative right to expensive assistance to do so.[27] And is any such 'right', were it to be accepted, beneficial to women? The desire to bear a child is a powerful instinct. The joy of motherhood is beyond expression for many mothers. But it is not the only desire or joy open to women. There are times today when those who speak publicly on infertility seem to propose a view that only via childbirth can a woman achieve fulfilment. That is a pernicious heresy.

What Parliament must weigh in the balance is repugnance against interfering with humanity and the affront to deeply held beliefs as to the nature of humanity, and the distress caused to individuals by infertility and, more crucially, the distress occasioned by families affected by congenital defects. For me at least the equation becomes: can the destruction of entities which are arguably human be justified by the prospect of reducing genetic disease? At present that prospect seems limited to screening and destroying affected embryos. There does not as yet seem to be much hope that 'sick' embryos could be cured and reimplanted to grow to maturity. For the present the task of justifying the destruction of the numbers of embryos necessarily entailed in the research process does not seem to have been satifactorily carried out.[28]

Workable and enforceable rules?

For law to command respect it should be enforceable. A further crucial distinction between abortion and research is that an absolute prohibition on abortion would not work. Women would once again resort to backstreet abortion.[29] Some embryos would be saved. Women would die or irretrievably prejudice their health and fertility. The laws on abortion would be seen to be flouted at a terrible cost to the 'criminals'. Nor, realistically, would the woman herself now be likely to be prosecuted. That kind of risk of mass disobedience of the law is not inherent in banning or limiting research. The Unborn children (Protection) Bill certainly induced Professor Edwards to state that that was a law he 'would be delighted to break'.[30] His defiance of the law though was aimed not at the central prohibition on research entailed in that Bill, but at the requirement that he must disclose a patient's name to the Secretary of State for him to authorize her treatment as part of any IVF programme.[31]

No such mandatory breach of confidentiality is demanded by the White Paper's proposals. Under Option A it is simply made a criminal offence to carry out any procedure on a human embryo other than those related to IVF treatment. There are no specific proposals to 'police' either Option A or B. Perhaps supporters of Mr Powell's original Bill see this as a weakness. Scientists, it might be argued, will simply carry on prohibited research under the cover of legitimate fertility services. That contention is invalid: first because it is rather insulting to those presently involved in research, and second because any breach of the rules if it comes to light will result both in the loss of the licence to provide infertility services and in criminal prosecution. The obnoxious interference in the doctor/patient relationship contained in the Powell Bill was unnecessary and counterproductive.

As far as the present proposals in the White Paper are concerned the extent to which the criminal law is deployed to enforce limitations on research under Option B is a matter of greater concern. Several procedures will constitute criminal offences. Not only will it be a crime to experiment on an embryo save under licence from the SLA, the following procedures will also attract criminal penalties: any research beyond the fourteen-day limit, any attempt at cloning or the creation of a hybrid, or trans-species fertilization beyond the two-cell stage. Is this over-kill? Prohibition of research except research licensed by the SLA limits research to licensed and verifiable clinics. That restriction is justifiably enforced by the criminal law and detection and prosecution will not be over-problematical in such cases. The sanction of loss of the licence for engaging in prohibited research or exceeding the fourteen-day limit is surely sufficient to deter such research. Criminalizing those procedures seems to be largely a publicity exercise to assure the public and Parliament that researchers will not be allowed to slide down the 'slippery slope' towards creation of a master race or sub-human species. It is neither necessary nor likely to be effective.[32]

Conclusions

The initial debate in the House of Commons on the White Paper[33] was encouraging in that Honourable Members manifested a degree of courtesy and mutual respect for deeply held conviction all too often absent in that august place. It was profoundly discouraging in that neither proponents nor opponents of research addressed the fundamental nature of humanity and its implications for legal protection of the embryo. Opponents of experimentation closed their eyes to the implications of banning research on infertility treatment. They refuse to recognize, at least publicly, that prohibiting research necessarily damaged the IVF programme.[34] Proponents fell readily into the false equation of research and abortion. Jo Richardson MP[35] challenged those who oppose experiments to explain how the law can rationally ban research and yet permit abortion on embryos of more than fourteen days' gestation. Emotion permeated the debate. It was a tool invoked far more often by those MPs supporting lawful research than by the prohibitionists. The grief and misery of infertility was eloquently called in aid to persuade the House to elect for Option B. The 'right' to found a family was taken as self-evident.[36] No vote was taken although the general tenor of the debate seemed to favour Option B.

Whatever Parliament decides when Members finally debate the Bill deriving from the White Paper, that decision will not conclude the debate on embryo experimentation. Should Option A be implemented banning experimentation pressure will mount for its repeal. For whatever the United Kingdom elects to do research will continue elsewhere. And if more generous limits than Option B are permitted abroad British scientists will seek to extend the limit here. The techniques developed largely by British doctors and scientists cannot be 'disinvented'.[37] Yet hard though it is to frustrate the expectations of those from this country who have led the field in developing IVF, that consideration should not sway Parliament. Parliament should undertake without fear or favour the task delegated to them and determine the fundamental principles on which the law should define the protection afforded to the embryo.

Notes

1 *Report of the Committee of Inquiry into Human Fertilisation and Embryology*: Cmd 8314 (HMSO, 1984).
2 Cmd 259 (HMSO, 1987) and see the earlier consultation document *Legislation on Human Infertility Services and Embryology*: Cmd 46
3 (HMSO, 1987).
  to a married couple as a result of AID with the consent of both spouses is treated as in law the natural child of the couple, should be extended to egg and embryo donation. See the White Paper para. 89.
4 See *ante* at pp. 50, 51.
5 See *ante* at pp. 118–19.
6 For the White Paper's detailed proposals on storage of embryos see paras 43–63 *ibid*. That Option A grants the embryo less than full protection was expressly recognized by William Cash MP in the debate on the White Paper; HC Official Report 4 February 1988, col. 1239.
7 It has been argued that prior to implantation in the uterus the embryo *in vivo* attracts no protection from the law at present. Section 58 of the Offences Against the Person Act 1861 prohibits procurement of miscarriage. Thus prior to implantation is there any 'carriage' of the embryo within the uterus? This contention has been accepted in the context of the legality of the 'morning after' pill and the IUD by the Attorney General in 1983; HC Official Report 10 May 1983, col. 238. For a contrary view see M. Brazier, *Medicine, Patients and the Law* (Harmondsworth: Pelican, 1987) at pp. 202–3; nor can the analogy between the embryo *in vivo* and *in vitro* prove particularly helpful in this context. Implantation takes place about 6 days prior to the 14-day limit in Option B. And difficulties of prosecuting for criminal abortion before a positive diagnosis of pregnancy is possible, may explain on pragmatic grounds the Attorney General's statement *re* abortion.
8 See the dissentient opinion among The Warnock Committee that '. . . it cannot be consonant with the special status that the Inquiry as a whole has agreed should be afforded to the human embryo, to cause it to exist, yet to allow it no possibility of implantation', *op. cit.*, at paras 11.23–11.30 and at p. 94. Those dissentient members contended for the acceptability of research on embryos which were by-products of other treatment alone. There is no provision made in Option B to reflect these opinions. Option B places no limitation on the origins of research embryos.
9 As Simon Lee submits in 'Re-reading Warnock', in P. Byrne (ed.), *Rights and Wrongs in Medicine*, at p. 52, King's College Studies, 1985–6 (London: King Edward's Hospital Fund for London, 1986).

10 As Sir Bernard Braine failed to do in the first Parliamentary debate on White Paper, HC Official Report 4 February 1988, col. 1216.

11 For research scientists the implication of the rigid limit is that, regardless of the progress of a project and any imminent breakthrough in research, exceeding the 14-day limit by an iota will attract criminal prosecution and penalties.

12 See, for example, M. Lockwood, 'When does a life begin?' in *Moral Dilemmas in Modern Medicine*, ed. Lockwood (Oxford: OUP, 1985).

13 See Keith Ward *ante* at pp. 111–13, and 'Persons, kinds and capacities' in *Rights and Wrongs in Medicine* at p. 53; G. R. Dunstan, 'The moral status of the human embryo: a tradition recalled', *J. Med. Ethics* 10.38 (1984); and see the speech to the House of Lords in the debate on the White Paper by the Archbishop of York, HL Official Report, 15 January 1988, cols 1461–6.

14 But see also, for example, J. M. Harris in *The Value of Life* (London: Routledge & Kegan Paul, 1985), who contends actual capacity for reasoning and self-awareness is a precondition of 'personhood'.

15 See Michael Jones commenting on the Warnock Report itself; 'Human embryos and the ethics of pragmatism', *Professional Negligence* 1.19 (1985).

16 Alton's Bill on its face raised the separate issue of the rights of the fetus at 18 weeks. A person supporting research on embryos up to 14 days could thus rationally support legal protection for the developing fetus at 18 weeks. Nevertheless for many proponents and opponents of the Bill what is at stake is the permissibility of abortion at any time.

17 Section 58 of the Offences Against the Person Act 1861.

18 J. M. Harris, *The Value of Life* (London: Routledge & Kegan Paul, 1985) at p. 117: 'Nor can it be morally preferable to end the life of an embryo *in vivo* than it is to do so, *in vitro*.' Presumably this moral 'rule' applies vice versa?

19 See further M. Brazier, 'Embryos' "Rights": abortion and research', in M. D. A. Freedman (ed.), *Medicine, Ethics and the Law*, Current Legal Problems (London: Stevens, 1988).

20 See *ante* references at note 13.

21 As has always been the case in English law: see R *v.* Bourne [1939] 1 KB 687.

22 As Lord Longford put it, '... there is no certainty in official Roman Catholic teaching as to when the soul enters the body. However, whenever it may enter the body, it would be seriously wrong in the Catholic view to destroy the fertilised ovum, because at the very least one might be killing a human person.' HL Official Report, 15 January 1988, col. 1474.

23 It would be ironic if Parliament voted to accept Option B on the grounds that the benefits of proposed research justified interference with the embryo, and those benefits proved unattainable within the 14-day limit.

24 See R. M. Hare, 'An ambiguity in Warnock', *Bioethics* 1.175 (1987).

25 See Robyn Rowland, 'Making women visible in the embryo-experimentation debate', *Bioethics* 1.179 (1987).

26 Universal Declaration of Human Rights, art, 16(1).
27 Suzanne Uniacke, '*In vitro* fertilisation and the right to reproduce', *Bioethics* 1.241 (1987).
28 It may be argued that preliminary research aimed at screening and eliminating defective embryos is a precondition of any surgery to eliminate and replace defective genes. Further evidence that other means do not exist to replace the use of human embryos needs to be forthcoming.
29 And rich women who could afford to do so will seek 'safe' abortion abroad.
30 At the lecture on which his essay *ante* chap. 3, is based.
31 That Bill provided as follows:

1.- (1) Except with the authority of the   Fertilisation of
         Secretary of State under this Act,   human ovum *in vitro*
         no person shall –   prohibited, except
         (a) procure the fertilisation of   for embryo insertion
             a human ovum *in vitro* (that
             is to say, elsewhere than in the
             body of a woman), or
         (b) have in his possession a human
             embryo produced by *in vitro*
             fertilisation
    (2) The Secretary of State's authority –
         (a) shall be given expressly for the purpose of enabling a
             named woman to bear a child by means of embryo in-
             sertion, and not for any other purpose,
         (b) shall be given in writing and only when applied for, in the
             prescribed form, by two registered medical practitioners,
             and
         (c) shall specify –
                 (i) the persons by whom, or under whose directions
             the procedures of *in vitro* fertilisation and embryo
             insertion are authorised to be carried out,
                 (ii) the place or places where any such procedure is
             to be carried out, and
                 (iii) the persons who may, in pursuance of the
             authority, have possession or control of embryos
             produced by such fertilisation

32 See A. T. H. Smith, 'Warnock and after: the legal and moral issues surrounding embryo experimentation', *Address to the Association for Legal and Social Philosophy*, April 1986.
33 HC Official Report, 4 February 1988, cols 1202–68.
34 *ibid*, Sir Bernard Braine MP at col. 1216; Ann Winterton MP at col. 1245; Ken Hargreaves MP at col. 1249.
35 *ibid*, at col. 1212.
36 *ibid*, Peter Thurnam MP at col. 1232.
37 *ibid*, Sir Trevor Skeet MP at col. 1227.

Bibliography

Texts on embryo experimentation and use

Austyn, J. M. (ed.) (1988) *New Prospects for Medicine*, Oxford: Oxford University Press.

Clarke, P. A. B., and Linzey, A. (1988) *Research on Embryos*, London: Lester Crook Academic.

Dunstan, G. R., and Seller, M. J. (1988) *The Status of the Human Embryo*, Oxford: King Edward's Hospital Fund for London, Oxford University Press.

Lee, Robert, and Morgan, Derek (1989) *Birthrights: Law and Ethics at the Beginnings of Life*, London: Routledge.

McCullagh, Peter (1987) *The Foetus as Transplant Donor*, Chichester: Wiley.

Walters, William, and Singer, Peter (1982) *Test-Tube Babies*, Melbourne: Oxford University Press.

Weil, William B., and Benjamin, Martin (eds) (1987) *Ethical Issues at the Outset of Life*, Oxford: Blackwell Scientific Publications.

Yoxen, Edward (1986) *Unnatural Selection?* London: Heinemann.

Articles on embryo experimentation and use

Caplan, Arthur L. (1987) 'Should foetuses or infants be utilized as organ donors?', *Bioethics* 1.2, April.

Dawson, Karen (1988) 'Segmentation and moral status *in vivo* and *in vitro*: a scientific perspective', *Biothetics* 2.1, January.

Fleming, Lorette (1987) 'The moral status of the foetus: a reappraisal', *Bioethics* 1.1, January.

Harris, John (1983) '*In vitro* fertilization, the ethical issues', and, Warnock, Mary (1983) '*In vitro* fertilization, the ethical issues II', both in *The Philosophical Quarterly* 33.132, July.

—— (1985) 'Full humans and empty morality', *The Philosophical Quarterly* 35.138, January.

Rowland, Robyn (1987) 'Making women visible in the embryo experimentation debate', *Bioethics* 1.2, April.

Warnock, Mary (1987) 'Do human cells have rights?' *Bioethics* 1.1, January.

Texts on medical and health care ethics

Beauchamp, Tom L., and Childress, James F. (1983) *Principles of Biomedical Ethics*, New York: Oxford University Press. 2nd edition.

Bloch, Sydney, and Chodoff, Paul (eds) (1981) *Psychiatric Ethics*, Oxford: Oxford University Press.

Boyd, K. M. (ed.) (1978) *The Ethics of Resource Allocation in Health Care*, Edinburgh at the University Press.

Brazier, Margaret (1987) *Medicine, Patients and the Law*, Harmondsworth: Penguin Books.

Byrne, Peter (ed.) (1986) *Rights and Wrongs in Medicine*, King's College Studies 1985–6, King Edward's Hospital Fund for London.

Campbell, Alistair V. (1975) *Moral Dilemmas in Medicine*, Edinburgh: Churchill Livingstone.

Campbell, Alistair V., and Higgs, Roger (1982) *In That Case – Medical Ethics in Everyday Practice*, London: Darton, Longman and Todd.

Daniels, Norman (1985) *Just Health Care*, Cambridge: Cambridge University Press.

Downie, R. S., and Calman, K. C. (1987) *Healthy Respect: Ethics in Health Care*, London: Faber & Faber.

Dunstan, G. R., and Seller, Mary J. (eds) (1983) *Consent in Medicine – Convergence and Divergence in Tradition*, London: King Edward's Hospital Fund for London.

Engelhardt, H. Tristram Jr (1986) *The Foundations of Bioethics*, New York: Oxford University Press.

Gillon, Raanan (1985, 1986) *Philosophical Medical Ethics*, Chichester: John Wiley & Sons on behalf of the *British Medical Journal*.

Harris, John (1985, 1989) *The Value of Life: An Introduction to Medical Ethics*, London: Routledge & Kegan Paul.

Hirsch, Steven R., and Harris, John (1988) *Consent and the Incompetent Patient: Ethics, Law and Medicine*, London: Gaskell, Royal College of Psychiatrists.

Illich, Ivan (1977) *Limits to Medicine*, Harmondsworth: Penguin Books.

Kennedy, Ian (1983) *The Unmasking of Medicine*, London: Paladin.

—— *(1988) Treat Me Right*, Oxford: Oxford University Press.

Kuhse, Helga, and Singer, Peter (1985) *Should the Baby Live? The Problem of Handicapped Infants*, Oxford: Oxford University Press.

Lockwood, Michael (ed.) (1985) *Moral Dilememas in Modern Medicine*, Oxford: Oxford University Press.

McLean, Sheila, and Maher, Gerry (1983) *Medicine, Morals and the Law*, Aldershot: Gower.

Mason, J. K., and McCall Smith, R. A. (1987) *Law and Medical Ethics*, London: Butterworths.

Rachels, James (1986) *The End of Life*, Oxford: Oxford University Press.

Thompson, Ian (ed.) (1979) *Dilemmas of Dying. A Study in the Ethics of Terminal Care*, Edinburgh at the University Press.

Townsend, Peter, and Davidson, Nick (eds) (1982) *Inequalities in Health (The Black Report)*, Harmondsworth: Penguin Books.

Veatch, Robert, M. (1981) *A Theory of Medical Ethics*, New York: Basic Books.
Warnock, Mary (1985) *A Question of Life* (The Warnock Report), Oxford: Blackwell.

Collections of essays

Hampshire, Stuart (1978) *Public and Private Morality*, Cambridge: Cambridge University Press.
Ladd, John (1979) *Ethical Issues Relating to Life and Death*, New York: Oxford University Press.
Rachels, James (1975) *Moral Problems*, New York: Harper & Row.
Sen, Amartya, and Williams, Bernard (1982) *Utilitarianism and Beyond*, Cambridge: Cambridge University Press.
Singer, Peter (ed.) (1986) *Applied Ethics*, Oxford: Oxford University Press.
Steinbock, Bonnie (1980) *Killing and Letting Die*, Englewood Cliffs, NJ: Prentice Hall.

General books on moral philosophy

Finnis, John (1980) *Natural Law and Natural Rights*, Oxford: Oxford University Press.
Foot, Philippa (1978) *Virtues and Vices*, Oxford: Blackwell.
Fried, Charles (1978) *Right and Wrong*, Cambridge, Mass.: Harvard University Press.
Glover, Jonathan (1977) *Causing Death and Saving Lives*, Harmondsworth: Pelican.
_____ (1984) *What Sort of People Should There Be?*, Harmondsworth: Pelican.
Lindley, Richard (1986) *Autonomy*, Basingstoke: Macmillan.
Mackie, John (1977) *Ethics*, Harmondsworth: Pelican.
Midgley, Mary (1983) *Heart and Mind*, London: Methuen.
Mill, J. S. (1972) '*Utilitarianism*' and '*On liberty*' in Mary Warnock (ed.) *Utilitarianism*, London: Fontana.
Nagel, Tom (1979) *Moral Questions*, Cambridge: Cambridge University Press.
Radcliffe Richards, Janet (1982) *The Sceptical Feminist*, Harmondsworth: Penguin Books.
Raz, Joseph (1968) *The Morality of Freedom*, Oxford: Oxford University Press.
Singer, Peter (1979) *Practical Ethics*, Cambridge: Cambridge University Press.
Tooley, Michael (1983) *Abortion and Infanticide*, Oxford: Oxford University Press.
Williams, Bernard (1981) *Moral Luck*, Cambridge: Cambridge University Press.
_____ (1986) *Ethics and the Limits of Philosophy*, London: Fontana.

Texts on theology

Board for Social Responsibility (1985) *Personal Origins,* London: CIO Publishing.

Congregation for the Doctrine of the Faith (1987) *Instruction on Respect for Human Life in its Origins and on the Dignity of Procreation,* London: Catholic Truth Society.

Curran, C. (1973) *Politics, Medicine and Christian Ethics,* Philadelphia: Fortress Press. Parts 3 and 4.

_____ (1978) *Issues in Sexual and Medical Ethics,* Notre Dame, Ind.: University of Notre Dame Press. Part 2.

Dunstan, G. (1984) 'The moral status of the human embryo: a tradition recalled', *Journal of Medical Ethics* 10, 148–53.

Fletcher, J. (1955) *Morals and Medicine,* London: Gollancz.

_____ (1974) *The Ethics of Genetic Control,* Garden City, NY: Doubleday.

_____ (1979) *Humanhood: Essays in Biomedical Ethics,* Buffalo, NY: Prometheus Books.

Greenspahn, F. (ed.) (1986) *Contemporary Ethical Issues in the Jewish and Christian Traditions,* Hoboken, NJ: KTAV Publishing House.

Gustafson, J. (1974) 'Genetic screening and human values: an analysis', in D. Bergsma (ed.), *Ethical, Social and Legal Dimensions of Screening for Human Genetic Disease,* New York: Stratton Intercontinental Medical Book Corporation, 201–23.

_____ (1974) *Theology and Christian Ethics,* Philadelphia: United Church Press.

_____ (1975) *The Contributions of Theology to Medical Ethics,* Milwaukee: Marquette University Theology Department.

Habgood, J. (1980) *A Working Faith: Essays and Addresses on Science, Medicine and Ethics,* London: Darton, Longman and Todd. Part 3.

Haering, B. (1975) *Manipulation,* Slough: St Paul Publications.

Harrison, B. (1985) *Making the Connections: Essays in Feminist Social Ethics* (ed. C. Robb), Boston: Beacon Press.

Harrison, B., *et al.* (1986) *The Public Vocation of Christian Ethics,* New York: Pilgrim Press.

Hauerwas, S. (1977) *Truthfulness and Tragedy,* Notre Dame, Ind.: University of Notre Dame Press.

Henry, C. (ed.) (1978) *Horizons of Science: Christian Scholars Speak Out,* San Francisco: Harper & Row.

Human Fertilisation and Embryology, Social Policy Committee, Board for Social Responsibility, London: Church House, 1984.

Johnson, J., and Smith, D. (eds) (1974) *Love and Society,* Missoula: Scholars Press. Part 3.

Kelly, K. (1987) *Life and Love: Towards a Christian Dialogue on Bioethical Questions,* London: Collins.

King, J., Lebacqz, K., Nahas, G., and Schroeder, T. (1980) 'The biological revolution: the ethical and social issues', in Shinn, R. (ed.), *Faith and Science in an Unjust World: Report on the World Council of Churches' Conference on Faith, Science and the Future,* Vol. 1, Geneva: World Council of Churches.

McCormick, R. (1981) *How Brave a New World?; Essays in Bioethics*, London: SCM Press.

Macquarrie, J., and Childress, J. (eds) (1986) *A New Dictionary of Christian Ethics*, London: SCM Press.

Mahoney, J. (1984) *Bioethics and Belief*, London: Sheed and Ward.

Manipulating Life: Ethical Issues in Genetic Engineering (1982) Geneva: World Council of Churches.

Meier, L. (ed.) (1986) *Jewish Values in Bioethics*, New York: Human Sciences Press.

Numbers, R., and Amundsen, D. (eds) (1986) *Caring and Curing: Health and Medicine in the Western Religious Traditions*, New York: Macmillan Publishing Co.

O'Donovan, O. (1984) *Begotten or Made?* Oxford: Clarendon Press.

Ramsey, P. (1971) *Fabricated Man: The Ethics of Genetic Control*, New Haven: Yale University Press.

—— (1975) *The Ethics of Fetal Research*, New Haven: Yale University Press.

Rosner, F., and Bleich, J. (eds) (1978) *Jewish Bioethics*, New York: Sanhedrin Press.

Schneider, E. (ed.) (1985) *Questions about the Beginning of Life: Christian Appraisals of Seven Bioethical Issues*, Minneapolis: Augsburg Publishing House.

Shelp, E. (ed.) (1985) *Theology and Bioethics: Exploring the Foundations and Frontiers*, Dordrecht: D. Reidel Publishing Company.

Siegel, S. (1978) 'Fetal experimentation', in Kellner, M. (ed.), *Contemporary Jewish Ethics*, New York: Sanhedrin Press.

Simmons, P. (ed.) (1980) *Issues in Christian Ethics*, Nashville: Broadman Press.

—— (1983) *Birth and Death: Bioethical Decision-Making*, Philadelphia: Westminster Press.

Teichler-Zallen, D., and Clements, C. (eds) (1982) *Science and Morality: New Directions in Bioethics*, Lexington, Mass.: D. C. Heath.

Vaux, K. (ed.) (1985) *Powers that Make Us Human: the Foundations of Medical Ethics*, Urbana, Ill.: University of Illinois Press.

Texts on law and medicine

Brazier, M. (1987) *Medicine, Patients and the Law*, Harmondsworth: Pelican.

Freeman, M. D. A. (1988) *Medicine, Ethics and the Law* (Current Legal Problems), London: Stevens.

Kennedy, Ian (1988) *Treat Me Right: Essays in Medical Law and Ethics*, Oxford: Oxford University Press.

McLean, S., and Maher, g. (eds) (1983) *Medicine, Morals and the Law*, Aldershot: Gower.

Mason, J. K., and McCall Smith, R. A. (1987) *Law and Medical Ethics*, 2nd edn, London: Butterworths.

Skegg, P. D. G. (1984) *Law, Ethics and Medicine: Studies in Medical Law*, Oxford: Clarendon Press.

Articles on law and medicine

Brahams, D. (1983) '*In-vitro* fertilisation and related research', *Lancet* 2, 726.

Davies, I. (1985) 'Contracts to bear children', *Journal of Medical Ethics* 11, 61.

'Experiments on embryos – permissions and prohibitions under the Infertility (Medical Procedures) Act 1984 (Victoria)' (1986), *Australian Law Journal* 60, 697.

Freeman, M. D. A. (1986) 'After Warnock – whither the law', *Current Legal Problems* 33.

Mason, J. K. (1985) 'Observations on the Report of the Warnock Committee', *Scottish Law Times* 39.

Parker, D. C. (1982) 'Legal aspects of artificial insemination and embryo transfer', *Family Law* 12, 103.

'Symposium: issues in procreational autonomy' (1986), *Hastings Law Journal* 37, 697.

Index